# Theatergarden

## *bestiarium*

**The Garden as Theater as Museum**

THE INSTITUTE FOR CONTEMPORARY ART
P.S. 1 MUSEUM
LONG ISLAND CITY, NEW YORK

EXHIBITION ORGANIZED BY
Chris Dercon

FROM A CONCEPT BY
Rüdiger Schöttle

ARTISTS
Bernard Bazile
Glenn Branca
James Coleman
Fortuyn/O'Brien
Ludger Gerdes
Dan Graham
Rodney Graham
Marin Kasimir
Christian-Philipp Müller
Juan Muñoz
Hermann Pitz
Alain Sechas
Jeff Wall

# Theatergarden

*bestiarium*

## The Garden as Theater as Museum

<small>INTRODUCTION BY</small>
Alanna Heiss

<small>TEXTS BY</small>
Mariane Brouwer
Chris Dercon
Dan Graham
Antje von Graevenitz
Johanne Lamoureux
Frédéric Migayrou
Naomi Miller
Rüdiger Schöttle
Richard Sennett

THE MIT PRESS
CAMBRIDGE, MASSACHUSETTS
LONDON, ENGLAND

"Theatergarden Bestiarium" has been produced by The Institute for Contemporary Art, P.S. 1 Museum. The exhibition was curated by Chris Dercon, with technical direction by Hank Stahler and project coordination by Véronique Dabin. The exhibition was held at P.S. 1 Museum, January 15-March 12, 1989, and traveled to Casino de la Exposicion, Seville, June 26-July 30, 1989, and to Confort Moderne, Poitiers, September 29-November 29, 1989.

"Theatergarden Bestiarium" was made possible in part by a grant from the National Endowment for the Arts. Additional funding was provided by the governments of Belgium, Canada, France, the Netherlands, Spain, the city of Zurich, and Goethe House, New York City.

The publication has been supported by grants from the Booth Ferris Foundation, New York Community Trust, and the Andy Warhol Foundation for the Visual Arts.

ISBN 0-262-04105-7
Library of Congress Catalog Number (to come).

The Institute for Contemporary Art, P.S. 1 Museum, 46-01 21st Street, Long Island City, New York 11101-5324, is a nonprofit center for contemporary art committed to the presentation of a broad range of artistic activities in various media through exhibitions and related activities.

Lawrence Wolfson, *Design*
Emily Singer, *Design Associate*
Susan Jonas, Carole Kismaric, *Project Editors*

# CONTENTS

# The Exhibition as a Zoo

During the two-year development of "Theatergarden Bestiarium," it was always understood that the project would be a living, changing, traveling exhibition, rather than a stagnant, traditional museum project. Through "Theatergarden Bestiarium," The Institute was interested in exploring important questions about contemporary exhibition making.

From its beginning, The Institute has had as its goal the production and presentation of exhibitions that propose ideas about living art and therefore foster collaborations with living artists. Our exhibition program is never fully defined in advance, but it encourages deduction, evaluation, and judgment in retrospect. This is also what the publication *Theatergarden Bestiarium* aims to do. Because of the experimental character of the collaboration between the artists and the organizers of "Theatergarden Bestiarium," both the exhibition and the publication are meant to initiate and provoke questions about traditional thematic and group exhibitions so omnipresent in contemporary art today.

"Theatergarden Bestiarium" represents the sum total of many individual imaginations—a layering of differences, twists, ambiguities—which emerges as a chain of implications about exhibition making that reveals the meaning of works of art. Both the exhibition and the publication are a web of propositions that deal with the past, the present, and the future of art as a model for society. As exhibitions and catalogs gain in importance and numbers today, what we need is a further destabilization of the distribution and presentation of contemporary art. That is, let us try to experiment with exhibitions and catalogs in order to defy their accepted authority.

We accepted a challenge when we decided to develop a publication that might extend the ideas provoked by Rüdiger Schöttle's concept of how the Renaissance garden evolved into the spectacle of today's exhibition. We asked ourselves how a publication might enlarge the museum public's experience of looking at art. We invited nine critics and art historians to probe the ideas behind "Theatergarden Bestiarium."

Rüdiger Schöttle's poetic rambling sets the stage and gives free rein to the reader's imagination, as it evokes a mysterious garden setting in which the past and future unite in a vibrant present. Chris Dercon, who produced and organized the show for The Institute, continues the story in his essay outlining the beginnings of the exhibition and introducing the projects of the artists. Frédéric Migayrou explains how a new idea of representation was set in motion by Louis XIV, who one day in the eighteenth century danced before his court at Versailles.

Naomi Miller writes about the evolution of theaters in Renaissance and

Baroque gardens. Dan Graham traces the transformation of the garden into theater, architecture, and museum spectacles, from the Renaissance to Coney Island, Disneyland, and corporate atriums. Antje von Graevenitz writes about monumental architecture that derives its meaning from its surroundings and discusses the influence of international exhibitions on the ways society displays its artifacts. Johanne Lamoureux provides an essay that traces the installations of contemporary exhibitions back to the picturesque garden and evaluates their assets and deficiencies. Richard Sennett and Chris Dercon discuss the consequences of the rise of the city and from it, a middle-class public for art. When it came to documenting the installation at P.S. 1 Museum, we were determined to avoid the common documentary portfolio that has as its goal the proof that a work of art was presented in a given exhibition in a given space. Instead, we sought to depict the relationship of one work of art to another as well as what this particular exhibition evoked for the spectator wandering through it. We commissioned David Levinthal to make a series of photographs about the installation. Marianne Brouwer discusses the city as a theater of memory and memory's value to the present in a poetic text concluding the book.

The Institute has always been troubled by the fact that because most museums and art centers are continually harassed by financial problems in a conservative world increasingly hostile to new art, they tend to avoid presenting what might be termed "difficult" exhibitions, those efforts whose results are at best unpredictable.

Large theme and group shows are and should be severely questioned as a means of viewing art. Group shows should be provocative to the artists participating, as well as to the public. When these shows are merely an assembled series of objects by artists better seen individually, the process cheapens the relationship between the artists, the museum, and the public. It is this relationship between the individual who makes art, the institution that presents it, and the public that views it that must be probed and questioned over and over again.

In some ways the task of the contemporary art organizer is more like working in a zoo than in a museum. The environmental problems constantly change, and one's responsibility is first to the living exhibits, and secondly to the public. The decisions about how one cares for the exhibits can have an immediate and serious effect on the lives of the animals.

Alanna Heiss, *President and Executive Director*
The Institute for Contemporary Art, P.S. 1 Museum

# BESTIARIUM: THEATER AND GARDEN OF VIOLENCE, WAR, AND HAPPINESS

*Rüdiger Schöttle*
*Translated from the German by Joachim Neugroschel*

Psychomachy tells the story of a garden called Bestiarium—a garden facing both past and future, shining down on us as a golden age—a garden with lakes reflecting the sky, paths leading to exits, and glimpses of grottoes, forests, and thickets. The Bestiarium is like a moving mirror that helps us experience the beauty of the garden itself.

## WHY BESTIARIUM?

This is a world of violence, struggle, and happiness. Here, the Desires and the Passions are the wild animals on which the Virtues are mounted. Restraint, Intelligence, Courage, and Justice hold the reins in order to guide the untamed forces of life along the road of human harmony with Nature. Bestiarium is like a natural motor that man employs, mastering it with his acumen and knowledge.

The entrance to Bestiarium lies in the future and reveals a garden that evokes Baroque and Rococo designs. We see three theaters here: a small loge theater based on Giuseppe Galli da Bibiena's conception. This theater has two lateral wings housing a directory. A tiered fountain leads to the main entrance, which is located in the center of the façade. The tiers are arranged so that falling water creates a variety of forms. The name of this theater is the Pheasant.

The second theater is a large structure on a rectangular foundation, containing a theater-in-the-round with rows of seats that can be rearranged at will. A suspended ceiling rests on a circle of pillars around the building. On three sides of the building, the spaces between the columns are covered with decorated wooden panels, the upper part of which contains a series of figures between high, narrow windows. At the entrance, the wooden panel is recessed, creating a kind of vestibule. The massive columns are unpolished black granite. The outside of the roof is mirrored. A rectangular plinth, made of blocks of raw, red granite, connects the building to the landscape by means of a tiered structure. The name of this theater is the Solar Table.

A third edifice, resembling an ancient Greek theater, stands on the shores of an artificial lake. In order to involve the landscape, the back wall of the stage and its white canvas roof are movable. During the summer months, performances are to take place in the daytime as well as in the evening. The name of this theater is the Phoenix.

The garden thus contains three main buildings that reflect the historical phases of theatrical architecture: ancient Greek theater, the theatrical space of the Middle Ages, and the loge theater of the European courts.

*All images in the essay are from slide projections by Rüdiger Schöttle for "Theatergarden Bestiarium," 1987-89.*

The conception of the theatergarden links the Baroque garden (Versailles) to the world's fairs that evolved during the second half of the nineteenth century, even if these two systems of (re)presentation are altogether different.

The final international phase of feudalism linked empirical knowledge and the conquest of mechanics visually to the castle, garden, and town. The garden lanes are perspectively fused with the castle façade, forming a larger unity that confronts the town. On a symbolic level, the town and the castle are signs referring to each other.

In contrast, the organizers of the world's fairs selected the Metropolis, such as London or Paris. In its national pavilion, each country displayed its respective level of industrial and intellectual development. The site was the Metropolis, and the demonstration took the form of commodities. A society no longer depicted itself symbolically through relationships with various façades. Rather, a nation exhibited itself as a one-way façade in the guise of exchangeable objects.

The pavilions were aimed exclusively at the public made up of spectators. Buildings were shielded by glass walls through which the spectator looked while simultaneously seeing his or her own image. The shop window appeared more and more as the basic medium of display. The idea of the Baroque opposition of castle and town was transformed into a self that was all eye. Through a window, the eye sees a world of objects linked to the reflection of the eye itself. The world becomes a fantastic conception of infinite visibility and exchangeability, a world in which objects appear like will-o'-the-wisps of ourselves.

The image of the self reflected in exchangeable things derived from that
face-to-face situation that created symbols. Against this historical backdrop, the site
and expression of a theatergarden should produce a new framework that creates
meaning. This site should be neither the Metropolis of visibility and inventory nor a
rhetorical utopia. The orientation point is the central city of Western culture, Rome.
The seven hills of Rome would be a good location for this garden as an expression, a
framework that creates meaning that lives through the many ideas and images of
human beings.

### The System of the Theatergarden

The system of the theatergarden is based on the cardinal points. The loge theater lies
on the intersection. One axis links a cascade of water in the east to the cinema theater
in the west. The other main axis runs from the ancient theater in the north to a
second entrance in the south. With the movement of the sun in the morning, the
waterfall is illuminated. In the evening, after its daily semicircular movement, the
sun slowly disappears into the lake, amid the hills. The golden light of the setting sun
is reflected in the lake, in the cinema theater, and in a glass wall that forms the back of
the loge theater. Along with the east–west axis, two additional axes run diagonally
from the cinema theater. One such axis connects the medieval theater by passing
through the cinema theater and the grotto island, ending at the ancient theater. The
second diagonal axis, leading from the south entrance, runs through the cinema
theater, toward ruins on the hilltop. The terrain slopes up lightly from east to west,
culminating at these ruins. A mountain chain runs from the north to this point; it
begins with low trees, shrubs, and streams, rising through a rocky landscape, where
waterfalls pour into the valley. These waterfalls reflect the morning sunlight.

The loge theater constitutes the central area of the garden. It is not set
precisely on the true midpoint; it is slightly off center. It is virtually an eye, peering at
the sun and the moon. The garden has a wealth of theatrical vistas that accompany
performances on any of its stages.

If we think of the present as an oscillation between the self and the object,
we see a stage performance that is part of a series in our ongoing contemporary
drama. In the theatergarden model, bleachers surround a large table illuminated by
the light that is reflected from a canopy at which projectors are aimed. The space is
like a movie theater, except that the screen is not an aperture leading to light;

instead, the screen appears underneath us like an artificially agitated ocean, an ocean forever creating new conceptions by means of countless images that keep emerging and submerging.

### A Brief History of the Projections in the Bestiarium

Images appear on the tableau of the theatergarden model, images that usually only converse in museums, archives, and books. These are ancient images, painted or sculpted, whose speech is mute for us today.

When we look at the table of the theatergarden, we perceive a series of images and sounds through which we wander, just as we wander through museums that are silent in the daytime. However, after a few moments of sensation, we are abruptly swept into the conversation of these images, which play a nocturnal game after the departure of the countless eyes of the day.

Picture the Louvre at night, without visitors, in the penumbra of its nocturnal mood, when the paintings begin to converse, dancing with one another in an iridescent interplay of fragments both noisy and silent, harmonious and dissonant—a kind of nightly orchestra that, caught in the projections of the theatergarden, plays a game invisible to human beings.

Today, we not only have this mute orchestra of ancient images, we also have media to keep the orchestra constantly moving: film and television. They transform the present proximity of ancient images into the remoteness of now in which everything is produced over and over, vanishing and then reappearing in a different guise. We may believe we are making these images speak, but what we really have is a mute adjacency that simulates movement.

In this modern image machine, images no longer arise at night to dance and speak and move iridescently. They are far away, in a different world, and they are spirited into the picture box only when we press the button. It is a mute world of images that converse with one another, far away from us. Thus, we yearn for the song of sirens in a different world, a song we can no longer hear. This yearning is captured on the table of the theatergarden, forever present and forever remote; the world of the Louvre, the Prado, Western movies—inhabited by human beings, animals, forests, meadows, steppes, rivers, passions, and harmonies.

On the table we see our many images, whose fusion signifies yearning; fragments whose coexistence turns the present of ancient images into a talking window and the remoteness of modern images into an active present. Speech and

action take place in an image fusion through which the Bestiarium will resound as a new orchestra of images. We are confronted with our vast image reservoir that gives voice to our yearning.

## THE IDEA OF IMAGE

Words, images, and things seemed to move virtually by magic. As if in a ballroom, human beings stood around a gigantic dance floor on which their own creations kept reassembling in different forms. Whatever they conceived and created multiplied on the spot and were plunged into kaleidoscopic teeming. Any one thing instantly turned into millions. In this way, a tiny bit could trigger enormous movements, and a constantly growing structure pressed the human beings against the wall. They stood motionless before their works, entranced by the never-ending repetitions, a condition that kept them both numb and agitated.

The kaleidoscopic dynamics penetrated into their souls, producing an inner space in which their feelings likewise multiplied. The slightest impulse promptly generated a chain of self-reproducing emotions; the human world consisted only of the tiniest signs, which settled like a film over everything and in which the present seemed immobile. The images, which were the basis on which man created, kept reproducing faster and faster. They engulfed him like a growing chain in whose iron his feelings were trapped. Object, form, and content dissolved in the observation of these microscopic signs, observations that were then transmitted to the devices.

The tide of reproducing images inundated the human souls. While the images multiplied, the building that surrounded them was emptied. Memory was transformed into mechanically recallable systems that were made independent by the kinetic energy of machines. The once-beautiful house with the many rooms no longer existed conceptually; instead, machines moved the memory contents. The loss pressed itself, by the speed of its reproduction, into human souls, evoking a sense of lack. The souls of the Modern Age had feelings because of this lack, which was revealed when they awoke from their trance. They knew they had been having bad dreams.

Of the house of memories, all that ultimately remained were the outer walls and the roof. An empty crate floated on the torrent of the reproductions, a torrent that pulled the souls away from their memories. Everything was hazy and always someplace else. In contrast to the restraint exerted by identity on their external being, human souls remained in a constant haziness that permitted no identity.

*Peter Greenaway, The Draughtsman's Contract, 1982. The draughtsman draws the garden of Compton Ansley while the mistress of the house, his contractual lover, strolls through the greens.*

*Ernst Schoedsack and Irving Pichel, King Kong, 1932. Kong fights a dinosaur in Hollywood's version of an archetypical garden representing the unknown, uncivilized world.*

*Hadrian's Villa, Tivoli, near Rome, 118–38. The garden commemorates the travels of the emperor to the Far East. The lake suggests the River Nile.*

# Many Dreams of Many Gardens

*Chris Dercon*
*Translated from the Dutch by Bruno Groeneveld*

In the City Park
Act I, scene I
GEORG: Good evening. How are things?
HELEN: Oh, hi. Well, so-so.
GEORG: I just wanted to see how you were.
HELEN: Hmm. That's good.
GEORG: How's art? Satisfied?
HELEN: (Tapping her forehead with her forefinger) Here! Huh! Art—is that what they're doing? Art is something different. That's not art that they're making. They're all complete amateurs.[1]

Currently, one finds an increasing number of depictions of gardens in the visual arts, architecture, film, and literature. Among the most powerful are Walt Disney's theme parks, popular since 1955 when the first Disneyland opened outside Los Angeles. Disney's four parks in the United States, one in Japan, and by 1992 Euro Disneyland, scheduled to open near Paris, make up the bulk of the Disney Imagineering Group's business.

The recently completed Parc de la Villette is a fifteen-hectare—compared to Euro Disneyland's projected 1,945 hectares—nineteenth-century industrial landscape north of Paris at the edge of the city's ring, the *periphérique*. It grew out of an international competition that began in 1982. Like many historical precursors of parks, La Villette was coordinated by one architect, Bernard Tschumi, but was actually a collaboration between architectural groups and landscape architects, as well as artists, writers, philosophers, musicians, and filmmakers. Among the participating designers were, initially, philosopher Jacques Derrida; artists Claes Oldenburg, Coosje van Bruggen, and Daniel Buren; filmmaker Michelangelo Antonioni; writer Michel Butor; and composer Henri Pousseur, to name a few. As a concept, La Villette might have been an inspired dream, but when realized, the collaboration fell short of many individuals' expectations.

Tschumi, like Disney, used the analogy of film in his design for La Villette: the park is a landscape and an architectural program, a theatrical *mise en scène*, and a movie, all at the same time. The landscape and architectural devices are laid out in sequences, like frames in pieces of a film. Sound accompanies one of the garden segments, and other landscape features, like bridges, cut across vistas. The visual effect reminds one of a film editor, who cuts from one scene to another. Theatrical presentations presented in historical gardens like Versailles have been replaced in

*The Gate of Hell, Bomarzo, 1560s. Built for Vicino Orsini, the atmosphere of the garden and its mysterious statues are reminiscent of a sacred wood.*

*Ferrante Imperato's* Wunderkammer, *Naples, 1599. The cabinet of rarities parallels the animal and human instinct to accumulate and to classify.*

*Michael Wadleigh,* Woodstock, *1969. The rock community's tribal ritual in a sixties hippie version of the Garden of Paradise at Woodstock Music and Art Fair, Bethel, New York.*

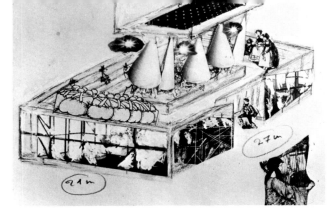

Rüdiger Schöttle, preparatory drawing for "Theatergarden Bestiarium," 1987, was inspired by the architecture of popular festivals.

contemporary gardens such as Disney's MGM Studio's Theme Park in Florida and La Villette in Paris by the dynamics of filmic representation.

Less spectacular than Disney's theme parks or Parc de la Villette, yet as interesting to the media and the public, are the contemporary sculpture gardens or temporary exhibitions opening in parks and gardens in the United States and Europe. Important projects in recent years include "Promenades" (1984), in Lullin Park near Geneva; "Sonsbeek" (1986), in the public park of the same name in Arnheim; "The Münster Sculpture Projects" (1987), installed throughout Münster, including the city's postwar reconstructions of vast recreational areas; and the contemporary art center recently opened on the Kerguehennec estate in Brittany.

In America the Minneapolis Sculpture Garden at the Walker Art Center, designed by the architect Edward Larrabee Barnes and landscape architect Peter Rothschild, opened in the fall of 1988. Paul Goldberger reviewing the garden in the *New York Times* observed:

*Ultimately, what makes this garden a potent architectural experience is the way the formal order of the Beaux Arts axis plays off against everything around it—the pond, the Oldenburg, the bridge, the expressway, the Walker building itself.*[2]

Goldberger sums it up: the park or garden in contemporary life leaves a more expressive or potent social impression than the works of art arranged in the space itself.

Why this revived fascination with gardens? Perhaps the German playwright Botho Strauss provides the explanation in the introduction to his play *The Park: A Play* (1985), in which the wood nymphs of Shakespeare's *Midsummer Night's Dream* are brought back to life and into consumer society:

*Imagine the following: an efficient society almost equidistant from holy things and from the timeless poem (and already a bit tired), succumbs to the genius of a great artwork instead of to a myth or an ideology.*

### THE DREAM OF THE GARDEN

However, we should return to the beginning of these great works of art. The imaginary garden or dreamgarden dates back to classic antiquity and was important to the Renaissance. Halfway between Orvieto and Rome, Vicino Orsini laid out the magical garden Bomarzo between 1552 and 1583, a dark, wooded forest which might have been inspired by the book of dreams *Hypnerotomachia Poliphili* (literally, *The Dreamed Love Struggle of Poliphilus*), written by the monk Francesco Colonna in 1499. In his garden

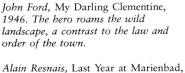

*John Ford,* My Darling Clementine, *1946. The hero roams the wild landscape, a contrast to the law and order of the town.*

*Alain Resnais,* Last Year at Marienbad, *1961. The geometric layout of the garden parallels the suppressed emotions and tensions of the film's characters.*

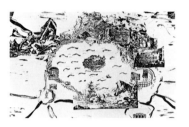

Orsini recreates the quest for the fountain of love by means of, among others, dreamlike creatures, *genii loci* arranged between the shrubs.

The shadows and private dreams of Bomarzo's love poem give way to a state manifesto that evokes a control of the masses in the open, sunlit lanes of the geometric gardens of Versailles, which Louis XIV had built one hundred years after Bomarzo. Versailles served literally as a theatrical backdrop for a continuous show that incorporated and demonstrated the power of the king.

Another one hundred years later, the political ballet of the king was replaced by the introspective *rhetorica* and *poetica* of the philosopher-poet in the garden at Ermenonville, north of Paris. Built between 1766 and 1776 by the marquis de Girardin, the garden at Ermenonville was designed as a journey, with a route charted between monuments and shrubbery that led the spectator from different chapters in the world of the Enlightenment evoked by writers such as Jean-Jacques Rousseau.

Leaping another hundred years or so, in 1894 Coney Island opened at one of New York City's beaches. The private dream of Bomarzo, the state manifesto of Versailles, and the poem that was Ermenonville turned into the billboard that was Coney Island, a retreat designed to lure the masses during New York's hot, sultry summers.

Coney Island contained three separate amusement parks: Steeplechase Park, Luna Park, and Dreamland. Dreamland, developed by William H. Reynolds in 1904, was meant to inspire Americans. It featured moral and uplifting displays such as The Fall of Pompeii and The End of the World.

Coney Island was the precursor of Disneyland, built sixty years later by Walt Disney on the outskirts of Los Angeles. Theme parks like Coney Island and Disneyland can be compared to the fantastic architecture of the world expositions and to the first open-air museums like Skansen outside Stockholm or Deerfield Village, erected by Henry Ford near Detroit. They symbolize the destructive impact of such inventions on the topographical mentality in that they dislocate and desynchronize the very experience of travel, inverting travel's time-consuming goal and its faraway destination.[3]

THE STORY OF A VERY PARTICULAR GARDEN

The exhibition "Theatergarden Bestiarium" has been derived from the text "Bestiarium: Theater and Garden of Violence, War, and Happiness" by Rüdiger Schöttle. The text is based on a collection of Schöttle's essays, *Psychomachia*, which he started to write in 1979.[4] In his text, Schöttle describes an imaginary theatrical garden in

Rüdiger Schöttle, preparatory drawing for "Theatergarden Bestiarium," 1987.

The medieval theater, called the Solar Table, and the nearby cinema theater.

The loge theater, called the Pheasant, and surrounding waterworks.

The ancient Greek theater, called the Phoenix, and nearby grotto island.

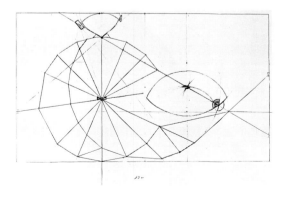

Eugène Atget, Saint Cloud, 1921–22.

Rüdiger Schöttle, preparatory drawing for "Theatergarden Bestiarium" based on the cardinal points, showing the main and additional axes, using a snail shell, 1987.

which the natural and the artificial worlds merge. The garden he envisions is essentially Baroque, a fantastic fusion of the Italian terrace garden, the French geometric garden, the English landscape garden, and the oriental garden.

In Schöttle's garden, the visitor finds, among other works of architecture, three theaters that demonstrate important phases in the development of theater architecture: the Pheasant, a small loge theater; the Solar Table, containing a theater-in-the-round; and the Phoenix, which resembles an ancient Greek theater.

Schöttle was influenced by the writings and works of the American artist Dan Graham, who in his essay "Theater, Cinema, and Power" analyzed the theatricality of historical gardens, including Versailles, as a catalyst for education and political consolidation.[5]

The structure of the theatergarden, as imagined by Schöttle, is based on the cardinal points. In historical European gardens, the visitor often entered the garden from the north, facing the sun. The eastern side of the garden, where the sun rises, was the female, life-giving side. The western side referred to the setting sun and the loss of life. Paths, trees, plants, statues, grottoes, fountains, and lakes conjured up stories or myths in the viewer's mind that were related to the passage of day into night, evoking a "theater of memory."

Schöttle's conception blends real images with psychological fantasies, creating a world of transparent, ephemeral photographic projections and reflections through which the visitor moves, at once as a spectator and as an actor. He describes the "Theatergarden Bestiarium" as being about life in memory and life in the future. As such, Schöttle's garden ignores the present or relegates it to the past or the future. Reality, or a democratized picture of happiness, as is often the case in dreamgardens, does not matter; what does, is a lively emotional present, emanating from the individual, not the community.

Dreamgardens were conceived or built far from the hustle and bustle of cities; or, if there was no other choice, they were located at the edges of towns, at the periphery. The construction site of Schöttle's garden is on the outskirts of Rome, near the seven hills. "This is the ideal place," he writes, "to bring into full expression the dream of the garden."

However, Schöttle's dream of the garden is also an occasion to invent, to arrange, and to direct an exhibition. The "Theatergarden Bestiarium" is as much a fable of a garden as it is the story of an exhibition.

The exhibition "Theatergarden Bestiarium" opened at The Institute for

*Marin Kasimir, preparatory drawing for "Theatergarden Bestiarium," with proposed tower by Jan Vercruysse, 1987.*

*Fortuyn/O'Brien, preparatory drawing for "Theatergarden Bestiarium," showing their "composite entrance" to the garden, which refers to a coullisse-theater, 1987.*

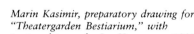

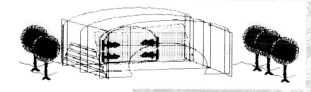

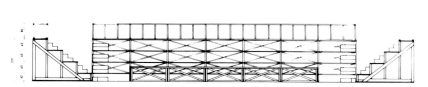

*Paul Robbrecht and Hilde Daem, architectural drawing for "Theatergarden Bestiarium," 1987, showing the viewing stands, table-platform, and projection ceiling.*

Contemporary Art, P.S. 1 Museum, in Long Island City, New York, in January 1989. From its inception, the exhibition underwent numerous modifications. How it was to be produced and financed evolved monthly, as sponsoring institutions joined the project and dropped out on a regular basis. The list of participants varied; the scope and scale of the design met with criticism, revision, and, at times, ridicule. In the end, thirteen North American and European artists agreed to participate and to create works specifically for the exhibition. How to realize Rüdiger Schöttle's ambitious but vague dreamgarden became a challenge to everyone involved: from the artists, whose desire to work communally often clashed with their need to protect their individual works; to the administrators who were charged with producing a one-person installation that was in effect a group show.

In most exhibitions of contemporary art the works are presented as a continuous collage; the visitor to the exhibition is not expected to be interested in any one particular work, but rather in the mostly subjective arrangement or classification of the works as a whole. According to the French filmmaker Alain Fleischer the same could be said of a visitor to a zoo:

*. . . you don't go to a zoo to see a lion, but rather a* mise en promiscuité *of African lions, polar bears, Bengal tigers, and Australian kangaroos.*[6]

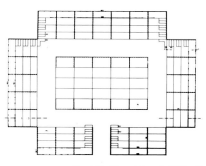

*Paul Robbrecht and Hilde Daem, overview of the viewing stands and table-platform for "Theatergarden Bestiarium," 1987.*

Exhibition organizers make no secret of the fact that the selection and arrangement of the works is an art in itself. Metaphors of traveling, landscapes, rivers, and other poetic inventions abound in recent exhibition literature. Such inventions or scenarios have become known as the "concept" of an exhibition. Obviously, there is nothing to stop the exhibition organizer from having an interest in literature. Kasper König, when asked about the nature of major exhibitions, said:
*In Godard's films you always see people reading books, which doesn't seem particularly communicative, almost as if the cinema public is being excluded. Yet in fact the very opposite is the case.*[7]

This approach only becomes dangerous when the works of art in the exhibition are subject to a scenario and a direction where the only objective is to express the concept of the exhibition organizer.

Would the exhibition "Theatergarden Bestiarium" also run the risk of being an example of these "exhibition neuroses"? Everything that transpired during the evolution of the project was, in a sense, an attempt to investigate alternatives to

*Koppel, the Ruin Theater in the garden of Sanspareil, near Bayreuth, 1746–48.*

*Michelangelo Antonioni, Blow Up, 1966. The public garden as a theater for the photographer-voyeur.*

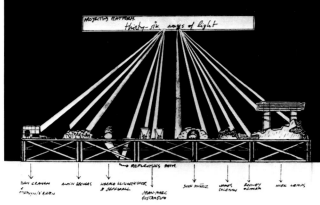

what has become the common, knee-jerk response to mounting museum exhibitions. Any original approach to rethinking exhibitions clearly resided for The Institute in an examination of the fragile balance between the authority of the organizers and the authority of the artists.

## FALL 1986

In the fall of 1986, Schöttle, at my request, first presented an exhibition plan, named "Das Kleine Bestiarium" ("The Little Bestiarium"):

*The topography of the designed landscape, in which the theaters and pavilions appear, is to be built on a table with a surface measuring about four by five meters. The model, emitting holograms and projections, is seen in the elevated center of a vast, darkened room. The adjacent rooms, conveniently illuminated, contain paintings, drawings, and designs by the artists, which reveal the decoration system of the constructions and the garden.*

A few months later, the concept and design of the exhibition had been adapted as the need to turn Schöttle's idea into an exhibition made itself felt. To clarify his ideas, Schöttle presented two drafts, or drawings showing the layout of the garden and the spatial configuration of a model. He described the project further:

*Twenty carousel projectors, set up on a higher construction, beam slide images down at the landscape. The projectors are combined with colored miniature spotlights that illuminate the theaters and pavilions. Lakes and waterworks are created by means of film projections.*

*The projectors and miniature spotlights are run by a computer. An overall tableau is produced by the various fade-ins and fade-outs. The variously illuminated landscapes and structures appear in the course of a stage performance. The model is shown in a large, darkened room. It is surrounded by an arena with wooden bleachers. The entrance, at the center of one of the long sides, is as high as the highest bleachers. The construction installed above the model looks like a sky that casts the light of the sun, moon, and stars on the landscapes and structures below.*

The artists listed in the description of the project at this stage included Glenn Branca, James Coleman, Ludger Gerdes, Dan Graham, Harald Klingelhöller, and Jeff Wall. With a few exceptions, they were only vaguely aware of Schöttle's plans. Schöttle and I, as the producer at the time, agreed that we needed to prepare a

*A view of a contemporary festival at Stourhead Park, Wiltshire, England.*

*The Electric Tower, Luna Park, Coney Island, 1903. Conceived by Frediric Thompson and Elmer Dundee. The amusement park, with its technology that imitated the natural world, was the victory of civilization over nature.*

Rüdiger Schöttle, first version of "Theatergarden Bestiarium," Kunstlerwerkstatt, Munich, 1987. On the table-platform was a landscape and models of glass and sugar lit with slides.

thorough project description that would stand up to intellectual and aesthetic scrutiny and answer the technical and financial questions that loomed. In addition, I believed the list of artists needed to be expanded to include people with whom Schöttle had never worked. BazileBustamante, Fortuyn/O'Brien, Rodney Graham, Marin Kasimir, Niek Kemps, Juan Muñoz, Alain Sechas, and Jan Vercruysse were invited to participate.

Rodney Graham, project drawing for Glade, executed by Neil Wedman, 1985.

### Spring 1987

P.S. 1 Museum was the first institution to express serious interest in Schöttle's proposal. Meanwhile, the list of artists was virtually complete, and responsibilities were assigned, in consultation with Schöttle. Whereas certain artists were asked to create a piece for a specific part of the garden, others, after considering Schöttle's plan, proposed projects that expanded on his ideas. Kasimir and Vercruysse were to work together on a plan for the "arena"—the area into which the garden's table would be installed. Working with a concept of bleachers and a tower, which was to be a variation on Vercruysse's *Chambres* series installed in various European exhibitions, they produced structures that would provide seating for the public and frame the fiction of the garden exhibition. On the table in the middle of the arena were to be works by Jean-Marc Bustamante, James Coleman, Fortuyn/O'Brien, Ludger Gerdes, Dan Graham, Rodney Graham, Niek Kemps, Harald Klingelhöller, Juan Muñoz, Alain Sechas, and Jeff Wall. Bernard Bazile decided for the time being not to create a piece for the table but to work away from it. Glenn Branca was commissioned to compose the accompanying music. Schöttle wanted the sound of a wind harp or a water organ to accompany his piece, which was to consist of photographic slides projected on the table.

From the beginning, virtually everyone seemed to question the concept of projected images. The authoritarian effect that the projections were likely to have on individual works troubled the artists. Another question that repeatedly came up centered on what the garden landscape, or the topology of the theatergarden, would look like. It was, after all, the landscape that would guarantee the unity of the individual works, the unity of the theatergarden, and the unity of the exhibition.

Most of the artists were attracted to the project by its concept of unity and collectiveness. How would the various pieces relate and at the same time stand on their own? How would the scale of the works relate to the table, the arena, the exhibition space, and ultimately the exhibition concept? Therefore, I asked the artist

Jean-Luc Godard, Passion, 1982. In his film, Godard comments on "the cinema of exhibition and the exhibition of cinema."

Joseph Paxton, Crystal Palace, Hyde Park, London, 1851.

Christian-Philipp Müller, who had just completed an intriguing reconstruction of a historical garden in Düsseldorf, to submit a landscape proposal that I hoped would reflect the artists' concerns. Schöttle doubted whether this initiative was likely to be useful; he believed he had been clear in detailing the appearance of the landscape. Spelling his plan out further, Schöttle believed, would only deaden the possibilities for each artist's imagination to work.

The design and construction of the bleachers and the table were assigned to the Belgian architects Hilde Daem and Paul Robbrecht, who had worked in Ghent and Amsterdam on architectural problems related to exhibitions.

### SUMMER 1987

During the summer of 1987 a meeting between Schöttle, the artists, architects, technicians, and organizers was scheduled in Münster during the opening of "The Münster Sculpture Projects," in which Dan Graham, Ludger Gerdes, Harald Klingelhöller, and Rodney Graham were participating. It was the first opportunity for everyone to meet and to begin serious collaboration.

During the Münster meeting, it became clear that cooperation between the participants was not going to be easy. A design submitted by Daem and Robbrecht was discussed; some artists feared their scheme for the table and bleachers would make for an exhibition that was "overly designed," and too expensive. Daem and Robbrecht reacted with disappointment and stressed that their design was meant more as a selfless support for the artists' works than as an autonomous contribution that would represent "architecture." They questioned whether the participants were capable of reading architectural schemes. Robbrecht stated his understanding of the difficult relationship between the visual arts and architecture when he wrote: *Seeing all these architectural images appear in art, the question arises whether the naked body of a woman is not inspiring anymore. That at least was the undisputed territory of the artist.*[8]

Harald Klingelhöller expressed his disappointment that the plan for the project was taking on an institutionalized look, making Schöttle's exhibition idea more ambitious than, perhaps, he had intended. Klingelhöller felt strongly that the personal character of Schöttle's idea had to be maintained. Gerdes doubted whether the exhibition would contribute any new ways to mount exhibitions, his primary reason for participating.

*Christian-Philipp Müller, preparatory drawing for "Theatergarden Bestiarium," showing the mountain range, waterworks, and shrubs, 1987.*

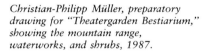

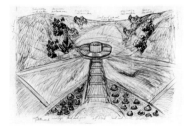

*Christian-Philipp Müller, Carl Theodor's Garden in Dusseldorf Hellerhof, 1986. The performance consisted of a guided tour in a new neighborhood on the site of a former Baroque garden.*

Robert Smithson, Entropic Landscape, 1970. The artist shows the transformation of industrial architecture into a natural state evoking the drawing style of Gian Battista Piranesi.

Dan Graham wondered whether the project could even be accomplished technically. He probed the character of the exhibition—the lighting, scale, and landscape—questioning how these elements would relate to the individual pieces on the table and how the individual pieces would relate to each other. Was the exhibition going to look like a scale model of a Baroque garden or a fusion of abstract landscape ideas? He believed firmly in the didactic, educational quality of the project and wondered whether it would be undermined by the process of putting the show together. After all, did we all want to make the same exhibition, or were there many exhibitions going on at the same time in everyone's head?

At the end of the unsatisfactory and inconclusive meeting, Schöttle agreed to perform "tests" on the table and the projections. In Munich's Künstlerwerkstatt, during October and November 1987, Schöttle presented in a darkened space, on a table supported by a light, metal construction, a schematic landscape made of sugar. The projections created a fragmented, hallucinatory, fragile image. I felt the improvised, unfinished installation did not provide a full enough sense of how the concept might be realized.

Meanwhile, Klingelhöller decided to leave the project. Hermann Pitz, another participant in "The Münster Sculpture Projects," took his place.

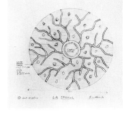

Robert Smithson, L.A. Sprawl, 1972. The artist renders the stretch of Los Angeles's suburbia as a configuration of crystal or foliage, referring to Rococo gardens.

### SPRING 1988

A few months later, in February 1988, Schöttle presented another version of the Munich table with projections, this time at the Maison de la Culture et de la Communication at Saint-Etienne. The presentations in Munich and Saint-Etienne, were both called "Theatergarden Bestiarium," and they began to create confusion in the art community about which exhibition was happening where. Was the "Theatergarden" project, announced by P.S. 1, already taking place? Our notion of defining the concept by working it out in smaller-scale, more modest installations was backfiring. Other colleagues began to react critically to the project. To them it was an unrealized exhibition, and the tentative results shown so far were highly derivative of the original concept made public in correspondence and in press releases issued by The Institute. This confusion led us to realize that it was probably best to say nothing about the project until it was realized. Again we were faced with another regressive idea about how exhibitions should function in the world. Whereas we had hoped to create an atmosphere in which the concept of the exhibition could be publicly debated as it was evolving rather than merely criticizing

Komar and Melamid, Scenes from the Future, 1983–84. The destruction of The Museum of Modern Art in a pastoral setting, referring to the ruin paintings of Hubert Robert.

the end results, we were being backed into a traditional museum posture: open the "perfect" show. As the machinery of producing the exhibition slowly ground on, irritation was expressed among the artists who were frustrated by the repeated postponements. Vercruysse wrote:

*I know that there were many external obstacles, but a project that has been dragging on for two years is no longer a good project. Artists are not a bus full of tourists who can be dragged hither and yon.*[9]

Colleagues and critics no longer believed in the artistic importance of the project, and because of the long preparation time, the immediacy of the subject also began to suffer. However, P.S. 1 continued to probe the content of the show.

*The Hunterian Museum, Royal College of Surgeons, London, early 1830s. Like Diderot's* Encyclopédie, *museums divided human activities into sciences, arts, and crafts.*

### SUMMER 1988

Proposals for the revisions of the landscape, sent in regularly by Müller, clarified how the garden might actually look. One of Müller's proposals was to cut through the table, following Hogarth's "line of beauty," a concept popularized by the English landscape architect Capability Brown in the eighteenth century. This proposed cut was to create a path for the public to pass between the artworks, entering, as it were, the theatergarden itself and becoming a part of the exhibition. Schöttle was still not convinced.

The project received a shot in the arm when the directors of P.S. 1, in spite of uncertainty, guaranteed the project would open in the winter of 1988–89. However, a budget review was contingent to making "Theatergarden Bestiarium" a part of P.S. 1's program. There was just so much money in hand, and The Institute had to make certain the exhibition could be realized for the amount it could allocate. Every aspect of the show had to be accomplished more inexpensively, therefore, more simply.

Schöttle, too, wanted to simplify and clarify the concept; so revisions began. The idea of eliminating the arena was the first decision made; so the bleachers disappeared. The lighting and slide projections were reduced to a minimum to cut down on costly projection and lighting systems. Although everyone had been committed to the idea of developing the show communally, a number of artists, it was disclosed, wanted a separate presentation of their pieces. Proposals along these lines went back and forth. Another group feared that the exhibition project would eventually become a conventional museum exhibition, with separate sculptures on individual pedestals, once again putting forth the sculpture as autonomous objects.

## FALL 1988

After Klingelhöller and Vercruysse withdrew, Kemps and Bustamante followed them. Bustamante wrote:

*This is not an all-encompassing project anymore that unites artists to work together reflecting the possible construction of a new collective work; rather it's now a presentation of isolated projects, traces, and souvenirs of a project which seemed initially impossible. . . .*

*For me, the garden, the organization of the table, and its surroundings were the very condition of this project—in a complete break with thematic exhibitions which are presentations of models. A break with the usual presentation conditions in order to produce an anarchic ensemble, kept within the guidelines of the initial proposal. The possibility of being confronted not with pieces, models, or objects, but with an almost anonymous work that would generate a new attitude. My original proposal could exist only if integrated within the ensemble, the sole unity of a place where the work "Bestiarium" came into being.*[10]

Schöttle also considered quitting. For him everything had taken too long. He had new plans for new exhibitions. In December he opened his first one-person show, "Wool and Water," based on Lewis Carroll's *Alice in Wonderland,* at the Victoria Miro Gallery in London, not as a curator or critic, but as an artist. Futhermore, Schöttle wanted to build a real garden somewhere in France. However, he visited P.S. 1 in November to survey the exhibition space and to work on a final layout for the show. However, it was clearly not the same project we had been working on for over two years.

Each artist received a detailed description of the exhibition space at P.S. 1:
*. . . The works will be placed on separate tables (not pedestals), constructed according to the specifications of the artists . . . following Rüdiger's elevation plan. . . . The tables will be made of plain wood, open underneath and simple in design. . . . Approximately thirteen tables will be joined together, but in such a way that the public can walk around in the garden/exhibition. . . . One or two features of Rüdiger's landscape plan will be designed, adapted, and executed by Christian-Philipp Müller. . . . Rüdiger's slide shows will be shown in another room. . . .*

Hermann Pitz responded:
*It is too bad we can't stick to the original concept of setting up all the projects on one*

*table. (According to the new plan, it would seem as if all the individual artists are to create curtain-raisers for Rüdiger Schöttle, which would certainly be overtaxing him. Oh well, it's your decision, you're the curator.) Another reason that it's too bad the original idea was abandoned is that I'm suddenly left all alone on a table surface, "of lumber stained to match the floor," and as you tell me, I'm not allowed to select the material [for the table]. So the garden idea has been given up? I suggest the following: the nineteen drops of water are to lie on the bare surface—and that's it![11]*

Pitz's reaction was understandable; after all, what remained of the original plan?

During the building of the exhibition in the auditorium of P.S. 1, it would become clear that everyone wanted to return to the original layout—a single table, a single garden, and a single exhibition; or in the words of Schöttle, reunification. The project was publicly announced as a work-in-progress.

### A COMPLETELY DIFFERENT GARDEN

The cover of the French paperback edition of Gustave Flaubert's novel *Bouvard et Pécuchet* reminds one of the "Theatergarden Bestiarium" story. Bertall's print, "Promenade au Salon," which appears on the cover, shows two gentlemen sitting on a park bench, enjoying their cigars.[12]

*Bouvard et Pécuchet* is the last, regrettably uncompleted, novel by Flaubert to which the author devoted the final six years of his life, from 1874 until 1880. In Flaubert's story, two lonely copy clerks strike up a friendship and decide to stick together in an adventure intended to unravel the fantastic, confusing world of the universe.

From the time they meet, the two characters exchange views on everything from government to the latest plays as they walk the streets of Paris. On one of their city excursions to the Natural History Museum in the Jardin des Plantes, they stare intently at the spectacle unfolding that will inspire them in their future adventure: *In the galleries of the Museum, they viewed the stuffed quadrupeds with astonishment, the butterflies with pleasure, the metals with indifference; fossils fired their imagination, conchology bored them. They peered into hot-houses, and shuddered at the thought of so many foliages distilling poison. What struck them most about the cedar was that it has been brought over in a hat.[13]*

Afterward, they rush to the Louvre, where they take in the magnificent paintings of Raphael. Bouvard and Pécuchet reveal to each other their dream of a

*Ludger Gerdes, Boat for Münster, 1987, for the exhibition "Münster Sculpture Projects." The boat is a reference to the tradition of water castles and gardens in Westphalia.*

*Mario Merz, Il Numero Ingrassa (come)
i Frutti d'Estate e le Foglie Abbondanti
0,1,1,2,3,5,8,13,21,34,55 (Numbers
Growing Like Fruits and Abandoned
Leaves) for the exhibition "Promenades,"
Parc Lullin, Genthod, Geneva, 1985.*

more adventurous, more informative, and, above all, more interesting life. An unexpected inheritance enables them to purchase a domain in Normandy, where they throw themselves into gardening, nurturing a reckless scientific ambition. In the library they eagerly put together, they find a book by Boitard on garden architecture entitled *The Architect of the Garden*:

*The author divides gardens into an infinity of styles. There is, in the first place, the Melancholy or Romantic, which is distinguished by everlasting ruins, tombs, and an "ex-voto to the Virgin, indicating the spot where a cavalier has fallen under an assassin's dagger." The Terrible is constructed with overhanging rocks, shattered trees and burnt-out cabins; the Exotic, by planting Peruvian torch-thistles "to bring back memories to a settler or traveller." The Pensive must provide, like Ermenonville, a temple to philosophy. Obelisks and triumphal arches characterize the Majestic; moss and grottoes, the Mysterious; a lake, the Poetic.*[14]

However, Bouvard and Pécuchet's projects and experiments only lead to hopeless confusion. The two amateurs have more trouble making their way in the world of science than they had expected. Tired and broke, they give up their adventure. They return to Paris to full-time copying, keeping a small garden.

The story of Bouvard and Pécuchet, so important to the world of literature, philosophy, and cultural criticism, is particularly relevant to the world of exhibition making. When asked about the presence of the dandified character in his painting and sculpture, Ludger Gerdes remarked:

*It is not so much a Baudelairian figure, it is more Schegl, or maybe a member of the odd couple, those restlessly searching godfathers of our times, Bouvard and Pécuchet.*[15]

It is no coincidence that Ludger Gerdes named one of his watercolors—in which the painter parodies the autonomy of the art object—after these two heroes: it shows two gentlemen with top hats, slumped on a couch, staring at the austere, dreary shape of some minimalist sculpture.

Gerdes, commenting on sterile exhibition art previously, had written:
*Just like in a botanic garden, works of art live in artificial spaces specially made for them. The work survives like an exotic animal in a zoo.*[16]

American art critic Douglas Crimp, in his article "On the Museum's Ruins,"

also referred to Flaubert's story as an indictment of exhi! :tion conservatism. Like Gerdes, Crimp writes a cynical commentary on the pretense of the museum and exhibition making. This is the image of the museum that is posed by Flaubert in his comedy *Bouvard and Pécuchet*. Crimp writes, quoting literary critic Eugenio Donato:

*The set of objects "The Museum" displays is sustained only by the fiction that they somehow constitute a coherent representation of the universe. The fiction is that of a repeated metonymic displacement of fragment with totality, object with label, series of objects with series of labels, can still produce a representation which is somehow adequate for a non-linguistic universe. Such fiction is the result of an uncritical belief in the notion of order and classification; that is to say, the spatial juxtaposition of fragments can produce a representational understanding of the world. Should the fiction disappear, there is nothing left of the Museum but "bric-a-brac," a heap of meaningless and valueless fragments of objects which are incapable of substituting themselves either metonymically for the original objects or metaphorically for their representations.[17]*

This is the same vacuum that is alluded to in Flaubert's novel, time and time again, not by Bouvard and Pécuchet, but by Flaubert himself. It is this same vacuum—"bric-a-brac" in museums and exhibitions—that "Theatergarden Bestiarium" attempts to challenge while reexamining the relevant questions: What is the goal of exhibitions? Why are they so powerful? Why do they have the authority they have? Why is there such an emphasis on the art objects rather than on the ideas that inspire them? "Theatergarden Bestiarium" strives to find meaning again in the act of production and not merely in the act of exhibition. As Gerdes has remarked: *In the art of the twentieth century, gardening hardly exists. A garden is an erotic situation between culture and nature. Twentieth-century art is autoerotic.[18]*

[1] Botho Strauss, *Der Park Schauspiel* [*The Park: A Play*] (Munich: Deutscher Taschenbuch Verlag, 1985), p. 9.

[2] Paul Goldberger, "Sculptural Links in the Chain of Urban Events," *The New York Times*, January 29, 1989.

[3] Edward Kaufman, "Created Communities: Architectural Museums and Images of the Past," unpublished conference paper, Center for European Studies, Harvard University, Cambridge, Massachusetts, April 1988.

[4] The complete *Psychomachia* was never published after its completion in 1985. Several chapters appeared under various names in magazines and catalogs including: "Der verlorene Paradiesgarten" ["The Lost Paradise Garden"], *Kunstforum International* (Cologne), vol. 65

(September 1983), pp. 68–73; "Das Leben der Ideen" ["The Life of Ideas"], *Doch Doch,* 1985, (Leuven, Belgium); "Drei Kapitel aus Psychomachia: Das Fenster zum Hof, Rameaus Neffe," "The Incredible Shrinking Man" ["Three Chapters from Psychomachia: The Window on the Garden, Rameaus' Cousin . . ."], *Ecco* (Munich), April/May/June 1986; "Psychomachie, Trois Chapitres: Jardin des Plaisirs, Les Jardins de M. Schreber, Atlantide" ["Psychomachia, Three Chapters: Garden of Pleasures, the Gardens of M. Schreber, Atlantide"], *Parachute* (Montreal), no. 44 (September/October/November 1986), pp. 6–8; "Diaphanie," *Au Coeur du Maelstrom,* Brussels: Palais des Beaux Arts, 1986, p. 46. Modified versions of the chapter "Bestiarium" were published in *Beeld* (Amsterdam), vol. 3 (June 1987), as "Theatergarden Bestiarium" by Rüdiger Schöttle, Munich (October 1987), and by the Maison de la Culture et la Communication, Saint Etienne (February 1988).

[5]Dan Graham, "Theater, Cinema and Power," *Parachute* (Montreal), no. 31 (June/July/August 1983), pp. 11–19.

[6]Alain Fleischer, "Portrait d'un musée ou la photogénie des lieux" ["Portrait of a Museum or the Photogénie of the Place"] in "L'oeuvre et son accrochage" ["The Work of Art and Its Installation"], *Cahiers du Musée National d'Art Moderne* (Paris), no. 17/18 (1986), p. 199.

[7]Kasper König, "De vraatzuchtige massa's" ["The Hungry Masses"], *Museumjournaal,* Stichting Kunstpublicaties (Amsterdam), no. 3 (1985), p. 143. See also Chris Dercon, "Art en Site: Art in Situ?" *Quatrièmes Ateliers Internationaux des Pays de la Loire 1987,* Fontevraud, 1987, pp. 8–17.

[8]Paul Robbrecht, *Verwijten* [*Reproaches*], Vleesen Beton (Mechelen), no. 8 (1987), p. 24.

[9]Jan Vercruysse to Chris Dercon, April 6, 1988.

[10]Jean-Marc Bustamante to Chris Dercon, October 17, 1988.

[11]Hermann Pitz to Chris Dercon, November 24, 1988.

[12]Gustave Flaubert, *Bouvard et Pécuchet* (Paris: Garnier-Flammarion, 1966). The references to Flaubert's *Bouvard et Pécuchet* were earlier cited by the author in "Marin Kasimir," *Made in Belgium* (Liege: Musée d'Art Moderne de la Ville de Liege, 1987). Reference is also made to the novel in Ed Taverne's "Architectuur van ontregelende gebeurtenissen, historische tuin en park van de toekomst" ["Architecture of Jolting Events, Historical Garden and Park of the Future"], in "Follies, De zin van nutteloze bouwsels in de natuur" ["Follies, the Use of Useless Architecture in Nature"], *Openbaar Kunstbezit* (Amsterdam), vol. 32 (July/August 1988), pp. 112–18.

[13]Flaubert, *Bouvard et Pécuchet* (Paris: Garnier-Flammarion, 1966), p. 39.

[14]Ibid., p. 71.

[15]Trevor Gould, "Ludger Gerdes: An Interview," *Parachute* (Montreal), no. 44 (June/July/August 1987), p. 13.

[16]Ludger Gerdes, "Einige Bemerkungen" ["A Few Remarks"], *Kunstforum International* (Cologne), vol. 65 (September 1983), p. 58.

[17]Douglas Crimp, "On the Museum's Ruins," *October* (Cambridge, Massachusetts), no. 13 (1980).

[18]Trevor Gould, "Ludger Gerdes: An Interview," *Parachute* (Montreal), no. 44 (June/July/August 1987), p. 12.

*Claus Oldenburg and Coosje van Bruggen,* Spoon Bridge and Cherry, *1987, at the Minneapolis Sculpture Garden, Walker Art Center, Minneapolis.*

30

# THINKING AHEAD:

## IDEAS, COMMENTS, AND PROJECTS FOR "THEATERGARDEN BESTIARIUM"

*Chris Dercon*

When the concept of "Theatergarden Bestiarium" began to evolve in the fall of 1986, the participating artists were invited to submit their first ideas for the show as drawings, photographs, or written statements. It was intended that these artists' projects would be an integral part of the publication, as they are the first manifestations of what Rüdiger Schöttle's ideas and texts of an imaginary garden provoked in each artist.

Bernard Bazile and Alain Sechas created autonomous photo works that are related to the very meaning of the words *Bestiarium* and *bestiary*. Dan Graham, Rodney Graham, and Jeff Wall verbally and visually deconstructed the meaning of the works they intended for the Bestiarium. James Coleman felt reluctant to present preliminary drawings or write about his work, so he invited an independent critic, Michael Tarantino, to write about his project.

The projects by Ludger Gerdes, Juan Muñoz, and Hermann Pitz have a personalized message; they are in the style of letters or diaries and describe the process of their collaboration. Glenn Branca, Irene Fortuyn, Marin Kasimir, and Christian-Philipp Müller in their contributions complement and extend the ideas inherent in their works. The architects Paul Robbrecht and Hilde Daem were asked to contribute a statement that would clarify the underlying ideas of their projected architecture of the space in which the art was meant to be displayed.

From the beginning, the projects were used as a point of discussion in the development of the exhibition. As the artists submitted their ideas, their drawings and written comments were distributed among the participants. As such, the projects are the first step in the realization of the exhibition "Theatergarden Bestiarium."

Bernard Bazile

*Valor Impositus*

A skeleton made from a plastic model lies outside a
vitrine, its bones in a pile on the floor. It is lit in a
manner that emphasizes the possibility of a drama that
has already taken  place or is about to occur. In medical
terminology, a skeleton is referred to as "articulated"
(reassembled) or "disarticulated." It is this process of
articulation, of giving meaning, of providing renewed
signification for the body's remains, that functions as a
way of defining the relationship between artist and
spectator. *Valor Impositus*, in initiating that course of
events and in isolating its personal component, locates
both the rupture and origin of drama.

     The vitrine is the locus of an exhibition space
that incorporates two basic properties of glass:
restriction of physical contact and release of vision.
Normally, the objects that are contained within the
vitrine are displayed in a fashion that connotes both
exclusivity and value. (The title *Valor Impositus* refers
to "assigned value.") These objects, fluctuating in value
and ultimately, in signification, thus become elements
upon which the spectator projects his or her vision in
order to put them into play.

     This personal projection illustrates the point at
which the activities of dramatization and fetishization
coincide. Sigmund Freud referred to the latter as an
activity in which a substitution takes place between
related objects. In sexual terms, this operation effaces
the unattainable by a trans- ference of attention to the
available. Like dramatization, it is initiated by the
subject or spectator. The resultant "spectacle" remains
both private and public. As Freud noted, "Its meaning is
not known to other people, so the fetish is not withheld
from them." In deconstructing the very process of
valorization—of both object and site—*Valor Impositus*
allows for the beginning of a *mise en scène* that is
ultimately directed by the viewer.

Michael Tarantino

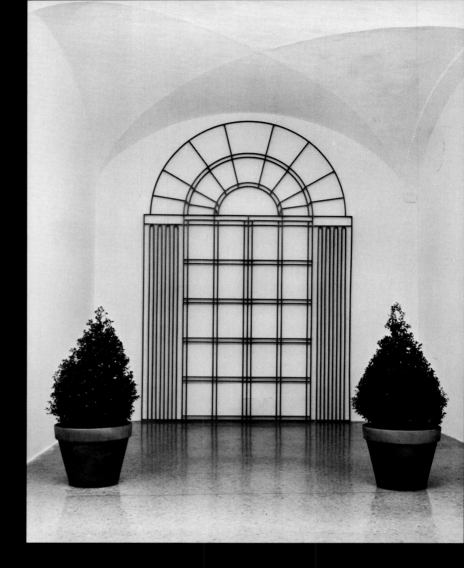

**ARCHI**

For your garden I would want to make the gate, not to close it but to make both sides more visible like a passage, a visual passage, layered—the opening, light fall, and hinges all on different planes, like lenses to be brought together by the eye on that one point where everything seems to fit.

**PALLO**

And then from the other side it should be like a
bridge, to climb onto and oversee the garden's
choreography, its pavilions, the waterfall, the layout of
the paths—all there for this visual wandering, crystal
clear in this filtered light.

Irene Fortuyn

## On My Slide Projection *Schwetzingen and Elsewhere*

My slide projection consists of four contrasting groups
of slides. Three of the four groups are made up of
black-and-white slides. The fourth and largest group is
made up of color slides. I photographed this color group
during several visits to the garden of Schwetzingen
Castle, near Heidelberg, in 1987 and 1988.

The garden was built chiefly under the regency of
Electoral Prince Carl-Theodor von der Pfalz (1742-99).
Designed by the royal landscape architect Johann Ludwig
Petri as a Baroque garden, the construction began in
1753. By 1776, it had been expanded by Friedrich Ludwig
Schell in the so-called English style. The castle garden
contains works by Alessandro Galli da Bibiena, Nicolas de
Pigage, Pierre Antoine Verschaffelt, Gabriel de Gurpello,
Ferdinand Kobell, Paul Egell, Franz Xavier Messerschmidt,
and other European architects, gardeners, sculptors,
stucco artists, and painters.

I photographed the second group of slides in late
1988 at the country property of the German sculptor Erwin
Wortelkamp, in the village of Hasselbach in Westerwald.
For several years now, Wortelkamp has been financing and
developing a sculpture garden there, with the
participation of other sculptors.

I photographed the third group of slides around the
same time at my studio in Düsseldorf, using various
objects I happened to find there.

The same is true of the fourth group of slides, for
which I received friendly help from five colleagues in
our studio building in Düsseldorf: Sandro Antal, Klaus
Jung, Ulf Rungenhagen, Christian Sehry, and Andreas
Wonkhaus. I would again like to express my gratitude to
them as well as to Erwin Wortelkamp; without my stay at
his country place, I would probably not have had the
decisive idea for *this* execution of the slide projection.

Ludger Gerdes

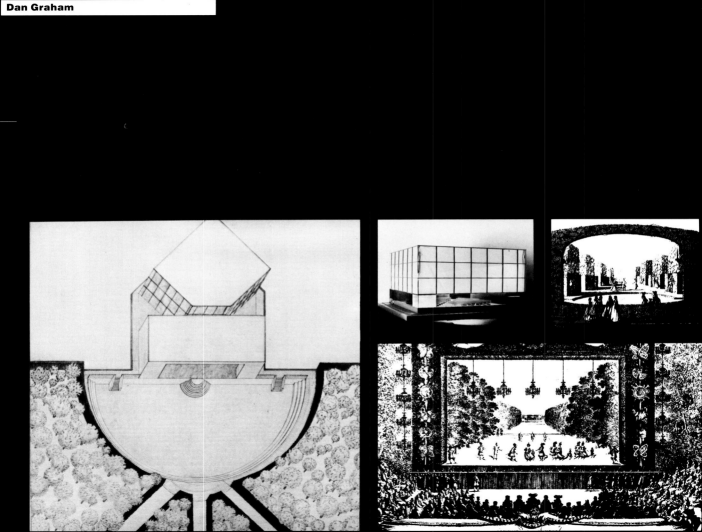

depicting an adjacent area of the same garden. The set's perspective is nearly identical to the perspective that the spectator can see from the area in which he or she is standing. The actors on stage wear costumes that are nearly identical to the clothes worn by the nobility who observe the play.

The rear of the stage set is designed as a two-way mirror that reflects the nobility viewing the play and the garden's hedge-lined *allées* as diminishing perspectives in mirror reflection. This rear stage set, as two-way mirror, also functions as a rear-screen projection, superimposing images of the film, Roberto Rossellini's *The Rise to Power of Louis XIV* (1964), being shown in the cinema. Two-way mirror mylar provides a normal—not transparent—screen for viewers in the "movie house." Because of the milar's properties of being more transparent on the side that receives less light, at moments of greater image brightness in the film, spectators *in the theater* will also see the faces of the cinema audience through the image of the film.

The scene used in my model of Rossellini's film shows the young king and his entourage of court aristocrats walking in the gardens of Versailles. The film focuses on Louis XIV's consolidation of his power through his reduction of the nobility to manipulated actors in a continuously staged spectacle. The difference between Louis XIV's era and our own is that royal stage craft in the seventeenth century was linked to theatrical representation. Today, political power and historical "reality" derive from the subliminal effects of film and television, which substitute media representations for historical memory. In the age of Louis XIV, the monarch's power was represented through his positioning himself by theater architecture and set design, so that all perspective lines culminated in emphasizing his position as the central point. His perspective was the ideal one: he was the viewpoint to which all the actions on the stage were addressed. Today, rulers' images are produced and manipulated in the way that a film or television actor is made into a "star."

*Cinema=Theater* takes the premise of Schöttle's exhibition, a return to archetypal German and European architectural, theatrical, and urban typologies, and proposes that today the garden as theater and as museum still does have enormous importance—but as an educational amusement park, influenced by cinema. The *Theater-Cinema* garden is based on the scenography derived from film's fantasy images and Hollywood set design.

Dan Graham

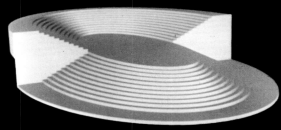

Christian-Philipp Müller

# Procul O Procul este profani

*Begone, you who are uninitiated! Begone!*

This inscription appears over the door of the temple of
Flora (1744-46) at Stourhead Park, England. The words are
spoken by the Cumaean sybil in the *Aeneid*, Book 6, as
Aeneas is about to descend into the underworld, where the
story of the founding of Rome is to be revealed to him.
The words were first inscribed in the early sixteenth
century over the entrance to the pope's private garden in
the Vatican.

Christian-Philipp Müller

*The Prompter*

Let's look carefully at the map. Rüdiger Schöttle pointed out the uncertain distance between the unmeasurable lakes. A little higher up, he showed me—or, perhaps, it was I who noticed, I don't recall—the image of a ruin. He suggested I might construct something based on that ruin. I had to tell him I'd come as an actor, awaiting the instruction of the scriptwriter, and the ruin, that analogy, was totally foreign to me. Besides, how does one remember something he does not yet know?

Rüdiger smiled when I made reference to the old blind Argentinian Borges, author of a garden of many paths that separate into two, and who imagined forgetting as a form superior to memory.

We began to speak about the ventriloquist's doll, of the image of the robot, and of simulation. At one point, I referred to the importance that dwarfs had played in the protocol of the Baroque court. Sometime later, or perhaps it was earlier, Rüdiger mentioned that the architect François de Cuvilles had also been a dwarf.

Days have passed since that afternoon; perhaps the events are now a bit distorted by the caprices of memory. However, I think I remember mentioning then a semicircular room, in the form of a seashell, without doors, and with only one window, from where, almost at eye level, a wide, long, ever-identical flat surface called a proscenium begins.

We looked through some books together. I began to understand Rüdiger. His illusory garden was like a theater in which there is neither audience nor play, but only a spectator placed in the center of the stage, reading the symbolic decor. The garden with its dispersed images forms the stage. To read these images is to be mistaken, again.

Juan Muñoz

Juan Muñoz

The waterdrops have to be executed in glass or acrylic in
about the same dimensions as a soufflé, about 10 to 20
centimeters high. They should lie directly on a surface
or else on some sort of textile, the structure of which
will be magnified. Since I was a child, I've thought of
waterdrops as magnifying lenses. The tautness of the
surface was always to me like a riddle. The magnification
has nothing to do with Pop Art. It's more about
clarifying the variability of this optical phenomenon
through changes in the vantage point of the viewer. A
field of 40 or 50 waterdrops will be formed to create the
image.

Hermann Pitz

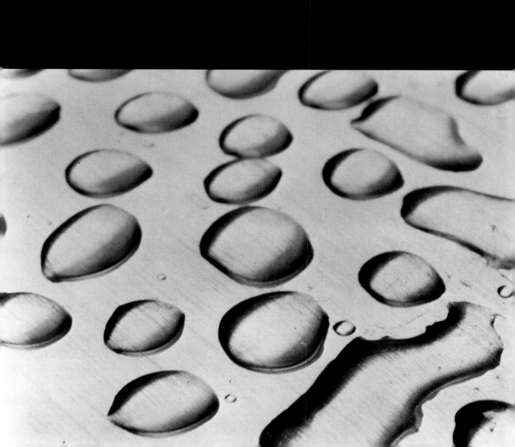

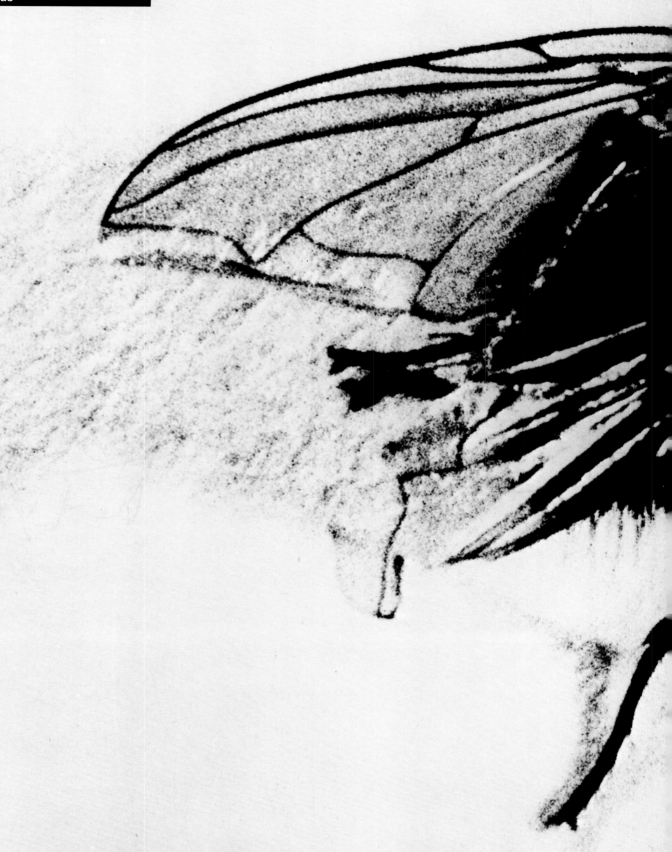

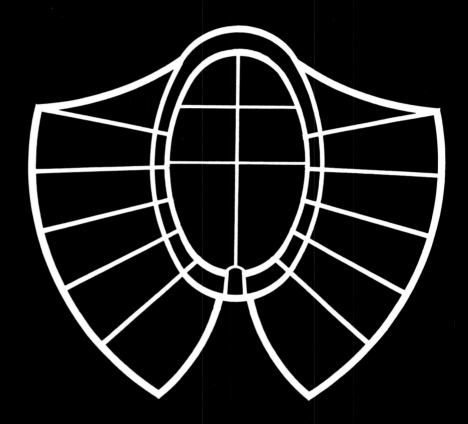

*Loge Theater With Its Plan Displayed as an Illuminated Sign*

The *Loge Theater* is an oval theater whose stage is visible from the floor and from four stories of loges. The ring of loges is surrounded by a complex of empty, open-plan model offices. The offices can be viewed from the rear of the loges, just as the production on a stage despotism, to which this theater type refers, these antechambers may have been used for various court administrative purposes by divisions of the state bureaucracy.

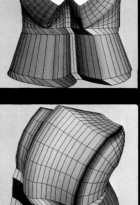

In concept, the *Loge Theater* exemplifies the historical moment of transition from court culture to systematic bureaucratic rule; that is, from a premodern, charismatic political logos to a modernized and objectivistic structure. In the culture of the Baroque courts, the notion of the theatricality of everyday life was common knowledge, even though the concept of "everyday life" had not really crystallized. If, in the Baroque, the office was a theater and the theater was an official site of political consolidation, then a structure evoking a reminiscence of this dynamic symmetry may evoke a historical memory.

The *Loge Theater* reflects a monistic orientation in its ground plan. Therefore, the exterior of the building functions as a support for a large, brightly illuminated sign that displays that plan as an emblem. The theater is a lamp, and the sculptural version prepared for "Theatergarden Bestiarium" has been conceived as such.

As the building rises above its plaza, it turns 8 degrees clockwise, throwing itself off the axis established for it in the overall design of the garden. At the top of the theater, the level at which its roof tilts upward 60 degrees, the structure turns another 8 degrees in the same direction. The protruded element carrying the illuminated sign twists 16 degrees in the opposite direction, thus placing the lighted emblem correctly over the original axis.

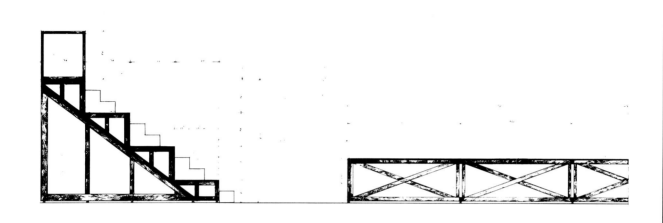

Under the Table/Under the Benches
Constructive Architectural Supports for
"Theatergarden Bestiarium"

It is nothing less than the visible world that is given
meaning by architecture. In the hierarchy of spaces,
attention is focused on the public areas: the spaces for
living, working, demonstrating, or circulating. In
contrast to spaces, a building contains unseen and
sometimes inaccessible places. These are functional
elements, and contain technical equipment or are simply a

"Theatergarden Bestiarium" reveals the function of
architecture to be the exclusive territory of support. In
contrast to the illusory nature of the art projects, the
position of architectural supports under the tables and
under the benches is very critical, and is like
architecture's own axiom: being for the good.

The terror that buildings often radiate shows the
precarious foundation of this moral objective—a question
of failure. Failure can be proceeded by ignorance or
negligence and can result in unforeseen prototypical
quality. Chance architectural practice deals with the
element of provocation. There is always the positive in
making a building—this compelled utopia, which cannot be
denied, ever, even when architecture does not aim to do
more than consolidate a present-day condition, or
speculates what present-day conditions could be.

Therefore, the act of building is normalized by the
acceptance of the extant, and in its way creates reality
for humans and animals. When an artist makes a work, he
or she is free to accept reality or not; it is the
artist's choice to project a moral attitude or not. This
rejection seems to be a necessity for some artists.
However, rejection, as well as rigorous consideration of
ethical implications in art, constantly leads to new
minefields of moral constraint.

In practice, the maker of architecture needs, as
the artist does, to rely on his or her personal
experience, states of consciousness, blind sense, or
conceptualization of practice. This difference
distinguishes architecture from art. A work of art
mediates these intimate layers, and in the effort to
bring them out of subjective experience, art gets its
importance and leads to common experience. In opposition,
the long process of building internalizes subjective
motives that are hidden in the masonry like secrets. It
is through the way the work is brought as evidence that
architecture gets its vivid anonymity, its available
space.

The hidden spaces of an architectural structure are
found in the foundations, in the walls, between the
ceilings, under the pavement, between a double dome, in
the elevator shaft, "Under the Table/Under the Benches."
In these spaces prevails a servile indifference toward
the world; it is the exclusive area of architecture as a
constructive discipline. These sometimes frightening
places are only visited by maintenance staff and
criminals, or by people with exceptional minds.

Paul Robbrecht and Hilde Daem

Scanned television image.

Leon Battista Alberti, The Proportions of
the Human Body, 1436.

# The Stage and the Register

## Everything Is Artifice in "Theatergarden Bestiarium"

*Frédéric Migayrou*
*Translated from French by Joachim Neugroschel*

How is the unity of a measure preserved? Can an order or the security of a standard still allow for the application of comparisons? At the start of this century, the measure signified the opening of the entire world, a proximity, a discovery. But for us today, geographic space has a global unity, the same extension as political space—an objective space in which the quantitative measure has eliminated the dimension of being—a space without quality, buried in a substratum to which we have lost all proximity.

*Rüdiger Schöttle,* Louis XIV Tanzt, *Kunstverein, Munich, 1985.*

When Louis XIV both watched and acted in the renowned 1661 celebration at Vaux-le-Vicomte, he did not reproduce the predictable static order of the cosmos, nor did he displace the divine order of the cosmos by analogy. His effect, and ultimately his power, were of a different essence; he gained his own ontological status, an original dimension that placed everything in a measured harmony, a closed and coherent world in which universal harmony reigned throughout nature, art, and the state."[1]

The composition of the spectacle and the figure, the *imagines,* constructed a new reality embellished with symbolic attributes that were not drawn by this theater of memory. *Iconologia* inaugurated the contemporary status of the image: the image was not the frame of a figuration or a representation losing its reference. Rather, the image *was the measure of a singular pattern—that of a universal harmony* (Marin Mersenne, 1636), *which would supply the order of any construction* (René Ouvrard, *Architecture Harmonique,* 1679).

When Louis XIV danced at the Versailles celebration, he escaped representation; he suspended all the arts as they were understood—the royal ballet, the design of gardens and costumes, the architectural reality created by the machines. He suspended them in a single gesture, that of a demiurgical transfer of the cosmos to harmony; a new order of justice, nourished by means of a previous voyage to the "kingdom of fairies."[2]

"Theatergarden Bestiarium" does not propose a return to the historical unity of the arts—an alleged basis for the system of representation. Instead, its goal is to affirm that the image is not born of the frame or of a configuration structured by the geometry of a distance. The human figure dictates the view in perspective of the garden; and tolerates a spatial multiplicity within its unity, arranging dispersed moments of time under the fiction of a new factual reality. The stage concealed the principle of its very establishment.[3] The viewer articulates systems of measurement through his dimensions—a directly factual image arising from an individual position. Louis XIV himself wrote the manual *Manière de montrer les jardins de Versailles* (*The Way to Show the Gardens of Versailles*). In this manual, he defined the order of the positions one should take to have a good view to embody oneself in the time of the promenade; the stations allow the stroller to measure the gardens of Versailles, the kingdom.

In the first version of "Theatergarden Bestiarium" (Munich, 1987), Schöttle's film images were projected on a miniature garden—a sugar surface—a screen garden; the viewpoint itself became the projection surface, and the projected image was materialized. The slides gave forms and colors to the landscape, in which the eyes no longer simply operated from a distance. In this installation, the unity intended by Schöttle transcends all issues of scale, so that the image is not a spectacle; instead, one can directly respond to the simple mode of the disposition of the image, making it the tool of an archaeological rereading of our systems of representation. The theatergarden thus opposes all analytical deconstructions of representation and performance, showing that each presumes a previous status of the image as a frame. A purism enters here: the juridical desire to rediscover underlying principles or else the acceptance of an historical plurality, a use of the quotation and the collage. "Theatergarden Bestiarium" lays down the law by demonstrating that this emerges from a common root; the normalization of space and time provides a frame for representation, a temporal continuity for history. Modern. Postmodern. "Theatergarden Bestiarium" indicates that the unity of the artwork hinges on its presentation—an active determination constituting nature and the city are both united in the artifice of the garden.

An exhibition has to reintegrate all phases of representation, whether that process is direct or indirect. The stroller through the theatergarden will halt in order to establish his viewpoint, a "station" able to organize all the scenes, stages, frames in terms of his relationship to the landscape in which he stands.

In Dan Graham's *Cinema-Theater,* which incorporates the scene from Roberto Rossellini's film *The Rise to Power of Louis XIV* (1964) when Louis XIV majestically advances near the great fountain of Versailles, the film projection bounces off a twofold stage, a cinema and a theater, in which two audiences face each other. Through a mirror, the image multiplies, separating the spaces but also creating a new audience, a community. Viewing is no longer produced by a distance but by an establishment in which the figure sets up the divisions of the representative system. The stage wraps around the figure; one is tempted to identify a continuous

space. "Theatergarden Bestiarium" displaces this relationship to its foundation of principles; it realigns the stage with the garden and the law with dreams, forcing the circle of totalization, of the frame for the image, of representation for power. It is the artwork that must open up and, in its autonomy, form the criteria of a judgment.

### QUESTIONS OF PRINCIPLES

In the garden, Louis XIV asserted his right to embody the world; he balanced all systems of codification that had been tried, for a century, to wrest a human order from the harmony of the cosmos. The garden achieved a universalization that could not yet be realized by the timid efforts at gathering knowledge (François de La Mothe Le Vayer). When, as shown by the art historian Erwin Panofsky, all disciplines, especially architecture, reconstrued the ancients, they distorted the Neoplatonic theory of the idea. This new understanding transcended the translation of the interior structure of the world in order to impose a theory of proportion, the passage from canonical rules to empirically functional rules.

It was Louis XIV who positioned the subject at the frontier of order. In the eighteenth century, that process led to "regarding the principles of natural expression as a limit of the very idea of convention."[4] The theatergarden culminated in an evolution of orderliness, in which man submitted to a world formed by his proportion—a proportion that would define the unity of the other arts. Leon Battista Alberti's man, the standard of a measure that had its correspondence in architecture, painting, sculpture, as well as in the city, reached his perfection in Louis XIV by forming a prime and absolute subjectivity. The king embodied a total individual, who unified the mimetics—a "solar figure" whose bared leg, the flesh of his private person, reduced everything to a common nature, the very place for exercising his power: the body.

*Francesco Colonna,* The Dreamed Love Struggle of Poliphilus, *1499.*

The urge for an overall codification of disciplines in the seventeenth century set up the rule and its subject with a single gesture. This development anticipated the formation of the private person, who, in the eighteenth century, opened up the public sphere as a domain of expression. The establishment of the Cartesian subject launched the era of rules that affected all disciplines: literature as dictated by François de Malherbe; aesthetics as ordained by Nicolas Boileau; the specification of a unity of the body politic by G. Coquille's *Discourse on the French Estates* in 1603; theater according to Jean Baptiste Racine; the grammar of the seigneur de Vaugelas; architecture with Claude Perrault's definition of "orders"—the list could go on.

This subjectivity essentially functioned as nature, the artifice of a world entirely ordered by rules that involved how it was structured, its "good formation" rather than its method of usage. The garden came before the Encyclopédie, because the garden presented a universality in which the subject had no place to retreat. In the garden, knowledge and technology still directly corresponded to the objects they created. The subject could exist only in the extension of the garden—that is, on the same ontological level.

In the *Treatise on Gardening According to the Reasons of Art and Nature* (1638), Jacques Boyceau defined the order of Versailles so precisely that André Lenôtre, the designer of the gardens of Versailles, decided to write nothing himself. Boyceau drew up two opposing sets of "reasons": those that dictate the quality of the elements; and those of art, "reducing on a large Scale the same Things that we have design'd on a small Scale."[5] According to the laws of the artist-gardener, nature becomes a machine object to be mastered by technicians, a theater, a décor with its grounds and backgrounds, in which architecture manifests the structure of the new perspective. Boyceau gave the garden the principle of codification, a relationship to nature, which unified the arts in a completely physical universality. The garden is a stage on which the normalization of the arts is inscribed, on which the poetic and the political remain indiscernible, on which the law is not yet inscribed in the register, and knowledge is not yet recorded in the Encyclopédie.

In "Theatergarden Bestiarium," Bernard Bazile's book *Antiphonary* has no content: it is a fluttering leaf, a bird in the sky of a child's drawing. Bazile's garden, the stage, derives from sound, not writing; making game of allegorical nature, where the monster can attack order like the serpent in the garden of Eden. In our everyday lives, the proximity to inscription is replaced by the functionality of plans—law, written texts—in which territory yields to the material of a cheap maquette. Bazile's pedestal supports this vacuity of inscription. The inscription is again subsumed in the vulgarity of the décor; the word gives way to song. The book accepts the alternation of voices, "the difference of voices,"[6] a gathering of works, of partners, whereby the theatergarden is no longer the prerequisite frame for an installation.

### ESTABLISHING THE MOTIF

Glenn Branca's music *Bestiarium* syncopates the stroll through the exhibition, creating the illusion of a continuity of time, a unity of displacement in space. The motif intervenes in specific places; it is no longer tied to the architecture of the whole.

*Astronaut Edwin Aldrin walks on the moon during the* Apollo 2 Mission, *1969.*

*Nam June Paik,* Something Pacific, *installation at the campus of the University of California, San Diego, 1986.*

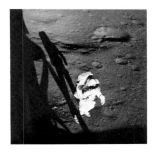

However, this autonomy of the musical might lead one to think that "Theatergarden Bestiarium" adapts itself to a dispersal of historical elements, to the fragmentariness devolving upon the artist or established as a new domain of the Baroque by contemporary semiology. Baroque: this is the critique that will map out any understanding of "Theatergarden Bestiarium." Baroque: for a purism issuing from a debatable reading of Minimalism. Baroque: for an Expressionism that is desperately in need of a unity of production guaranteed by a style. And, last but not least, Baroque for an art of the simulacrum, which will see a certain materialist heaviness in the presented works, a lack of economy in communication. Contemporary aesthetics always strives for originality, for unique works, pure "originals," and even the appropriation of industrial objects, the various presentations of contemporary art reinforce this symbolic value.

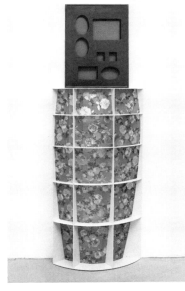

*Fortuyn/O'Brien,* For Those Who Have Tried, *1986.*

"Theatergarden Bestiarium" is entirely bound up with the recognition of a state of aesthetics and politics in which the systems of representation are completely occupied by variation and the relationship of works to one another. In this exhibit, the fragmentation and irregularity of present-day culture confront the indecisiveness of a historical separation that did not distinguish between the Baroque and classicism. This is not a return to a hypothetical modern foundation, a primary tabula rasa, the "quarrel between the ancients and the moderns," echoed by the breakup of the avant-gardes.

The Theatrum Mundi, the "World's Theater" of the Baroque vision, as invoked by Schöttle, has not yet closed up into a totality; it does not create hierarchies; the subject has the same value as its origin, the décor the same value as the structure. "Theatergarden Bestiarium" is a matrix that allows us to subsume the most disparate visual fragments of the universe under the same realization. Images from movies, TV, and photographs yield to the rule of a reading in which the detail has the same value as the whole; a reading that introduces a rule of reading that no longer invokes the nostalgia for an original; a reading in which a renunciation faces the dissolution of images. The aesthetic ideal produced by Romanticism, reinforced by the avant-gardes, preserved by the cultural anthropology of the media, now appears in its impossible relationship to the totality—a vision of the world. In "Theatergarden Bestiarium," the motif gains total autonomy, escaping the Rococo, the exhaustion of ornamentation, and finding its place in an order of which the subject matter itself is the agent. The motif becomes a figure, and this is what distinguished the geometric garden arising from the Renaissance of the theatergarden. René Descartes versus Gérard Desargues, analytical geometry versus plane geometry. Shifting the geometric order to the search for invariants between a figure and its projection means imposing the same value on the detail as on the overall structure. This understanding of space blurs the distinction between the Baroque and classicism. The classical order seems rightfully to belong to the same sphere as Baroque overdetermination—or, to quote Francis Ponge in *For Malherbe*: "Classicism is merely the tightest tightrope of the Baroque."

Ludger Gerdes's slide projections in "Theatergarden Bestiarium" play with the permanent shift between motif, figure, and foundation and make them clash with the static position of the contemporary spectator. The projections intertwine, endlessly shifting the correspondences between nature and garden, construction and abandonment, present and past. By gaining independence from the ornament and the motif, the image must rediscover its function as a "visual narrative," its ability to "construct a place" ("places are to be understood as concretized narratives")[7]—a space that is not defined as a frame for our projection.

## The Dream, the Fable

The idea of utopia seems inexorably linked to the formation of modern political power, to the genesis of territory and its other, to the genesis of law and its transgression. By advancing the hypothesis of the theatergarden, we see the parade of a whole architecture of the utopian discourse, in which narrative hazily crosses the dream that arranges the geometry of the other place. From Artistotle's *The Republic* to Thomas More's *Utopia*—the literary parable of the other world was forcefully reborn in the seventeenth century and achieved an apotheosis in the eighteenth, because it was a token of a formation of the political, a figuration of a juridical mastering of territory, a geometry of space, of bodies according to a harmony of proportions.

Utopia is the revolution of a history; utopia is a country, a city, a garden, a dream. Utopia is a theoretical body that feeds the conceptions of history, the conceptions of the narrative and the sign, the conceptions of power. Far from being myth, utopia leans on a barely constituted and ontologically formed time, the time of *Philebus*, in which, with Plato, narrative establishes memory, a blank memory, a simple position.

The narrative remains the fundamental term of a unity of vision, of construction—not only because the narrative can articulate disparate plans, pro-

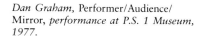

*Dan Graham,* Performer/Audience/ Mirror, *performance at P.S. 1 Museum, 1977.*

duced by heterogeneous conceptions, but also because narrative, in essence, is the very site of a formation of law, a "fictioning" of the Law. The fable, a prefiguration of the dream, reshapes the unity of time—a continuity, a totality that can be mastered, a human order against indeterminable animality. According to an Aristotelian tradition, memory offers a regulation of soul and body and forms theologically precise patterns of thought. Against canonical rigorism, the fable and the dream are possibilities for reintroducing anthropomorphic values in the ideal criteria, for constituting the form of a modern system of law for the individual. The dream, occurring in the works of Pedro Calderón de la Barca, William Shakespeare, and Pierre Corneille, was a Baroque motif, because it brought man closer to a new codification. In the seventeenth century, the dream was the key to a spatial metaphor, like the mythological countryside of Honoré d'Urfé's *L'Astré*; but it remained the favorite vehicle for shaping a new order of the visible.

"Theatergarden Bestiarium" considers the fictitious core of a subjectivity—the first subject that constitutes the surrounding world, the first conflict created by such a separation, the display of power in its exercise upon a domain that is more and more difficult to master. When James Coleman presents us with a vitrine, *Valor Impositus,* he is indicating that every stage remains empty if it is not produced by the active reception of the spectator. The description of Colonel Morris's uniform and his biography await actualization; the actual reflection of the spectator in the glass of the vitrine leaves only a skeleton at his feet, a figuration with no figure, the vestiges of the traditional historical representation.

### THE STAGE OF THE INSCRIPTION

The links uniting the architecture and theater, the power and makeup of the public space in the Baroque garden, cannot be grasped by means of a discourse on representation if that discourse has been stabilized and objectified only with its own crisis in the avant-gardes. "Theatergarden Bestiarium" never defines the garden as a framework or stage for a demonstration in which everyone would have to choose a place, a position. If there is a stage, then it is established only as the extension of a constructive reception of each work.

In a Baroque theater, the royal box was situated in such a way that the king could see and be seen. This articulation of the architectural space led to a separation of the audience in opera houses of the nineteenth century: the social hierarchy definitively determined the vantage points, stabilizing the audience's state of passive

*Bernard Palissy, La Belle Jardiniere (The Beautiful Gardener), Paris, 1580.*

reception. With the introduction of orchestra seats rather than a penned-in corral for viewers, the relationship between the stage and the inscription was reorganized.

Jeff Wall (*Loge Theater with Its Plan Displayed as an Illuminated Sign*) restores the spectators to the central place they had in the "station" of the theatergarden, but he does not spurn the visual production of the contemporary technologies of the spectacle. He accentuates the interrelationship between the figure and its extension into perspective. The belief in a representational stage waiting for an inscription is precisely what underlies the failure of the deconstructions—a quest for pure space, which presupposes that which it denounces. The multitopical space of a Baroque garden created by its extension into infinity and the reappropriation of the subject meet their limit in the imbalance of the human and its symbolic gestures—a mockery of the gesture of the first man on the moon. Wall reverses the proposition of the total theater that was born with the synesthetic spectacle of the Symbolists. When he sets up the theater box, the drawing of a social condition of the inscription in a lit sign in front of the public space, he reveals the form of this economy of power on the performance. In "Theatergarden Bestiarium," the stage, thoroughly crisscrossed, loses its topological assignment, sending the viewer back to his own position in the viewing. Similarly, Juan Muñoz's *The Prompter* accentuates the idea of a laughable marginality for the person who preserved the anthropology of a subject for the performance.

The stage is set in relation to the figure; under the fiction of a continuous time, the stage gathers elements from distinct ontologies. The establishment of the "tableau stage" presupposed a figurative sculptural object, "a figurative object that can, incidentally, define the place in the same way as the mere presence of a character,"[8] that anticipated the advent of perspective as a foundation and mastery of figured space. "Theatergarden Bestiarium" liberates this figural arrangement, leading the eyes into the material of the images—classical paintings and movie stills—fragmented by the interplay of mirrors.

Schöttle's slide projection impels the viewer to reactualize his position in the incessant movement of the projection, a cinematic collage that eludes history, memory, the unity of vision in the royal box, the unity of appearance in the performance hall. Thus, the moment opposes history, the aspect opposes the totality, the image is reborn from the frame that the public spontaneously accepts and recognizes. The stage of the inscription, with no possibility of withdrawal by the subject, offers itself as an empty space, at the outskirts of the Baroque imbalance

between distanciation and infinite extension, between overall vision and poetic fusion. The delimitations and symmetries that define it came from an architecture without a foundation.

Rodney Graham's *Maritime Theater and Staircase* attempts to fuse the architecture of Walter Gropius's total theater (*Totaltheater for E. Piscator*, 1927) and the ordered unity of the classical garden that gathers its elements. This fusion annuls all distance, bringing the gaze back to a finitude in which the image is blank, devoid of content, the stage of an inscription without a trace.

## THE NATURE OF NATURE

When Dezallier d'Argenville wrote his *Treatise on Gardening*, nature found its unity. Nature became an object that could be mastered. It grew thanks to classification and taxinomy. Nature acquired a spatial frame that awaited separation and orderly arrangement. It became temporal; it had its history, a natural history. Jean-Jacques Rousseau gathered herbs, the marquis de Sade pursued instinct, and, with the comte de Buffon, the curio cabinet yielded to the law of collecting. Nature had to be either constrained, put in order, or imitated. Whether it was an object of knowledge or a perceptible domain, nature was formed as an object of permanent reappropriation. Man established nature by separating himself from nature; he diversified it by his intent to assemble a totality. Nature was made up of correspondences, analogies; and the garden was a microcosm in which man spontaneously found his place. The theatergarden thus appeared as the link between cosmos and totality, a stage on which gathering opposed fusion and codification opposed necessity. Such is the meaning of Christian-Philipp Müller's piece *Toward a Beltwalk*. The theatrical tiers are also the terracing of the pots in the garden hothouse; the "natural" plant tamed by commerce is reduced to a stereotype, and refers to a different commercial object, a coarse leather belt, the parable of an assembling. The belt encloses the hothouse plants; Müller refers identity and totality back to back, the ideology of a knowledge that is historically tied to the deployment of mercantilism, the reason for an art object whose function is still divided between business and collecting.

Nature can no longer be that final object that escapes the normalization by the art market. But because the inscription in the territory of a Robert Smithson is now assimilated by institutions as an aesthetic act, Müller takes the rocks from an installation by Smithson and places them on a table as if in a theater stall (*Cinema Seats Dedicated to R.S.*). Nature has definitively yielded to totalization; it is merely a

Bernard Bazile, Le Lustre (The Lamp), 1979.

variation of its *mise en scène*. It is always within the frame of an image, that of a satellite or that of an urban planner tracing the trans-Amazon route. The general grid work of the public space destroys the structure of the community, accentuating the withdrawal of individuals to a private sphere, which swaps its autonomy for a new narcissism.

Alain Sechas's *Cabbage Without Roots* exhumes this seesawing, which, in the eighteenth century, inaugurated the retreat to the private garden (a ludicrous opposition between city and country), and which fed the worldwide spread of urbanity. The studded leather jacket, a sign of being different, marginality, the hooligan, the homosexual, and sadomasochism, is the standard of a culture of individualism run amuck, a global value mediated by films and rock music. Louis XIV, the first individual, had not yet separated nature and politics, reason and sensitivity. He began to do so when he was able to distribute the offices of a newly created public space, at the very moment when Versailles, at the end of his reign, was sedimented into a model of the city, an infinite extension. Alain Sechas attempts the absurd fusion between the inauguration of nature, as a domain of the sensibilities, and the most extreme artifice of a corruption of individualism: cabbages made of studded leather.

Everything is artifice in "Theatergarden Bestiarium": nature is sired by form, by the idea — a schematism that still has a difficult time dividing nature and the indistinct, a world of spirits, demons, and witchcraft. The vogue of literary fantasies during the seventeenth century was a response to the spread of rationality. The tale of wonder seemed like a sublimation, the exorcism of primeval terrors. Jean de Prehac's chapbook *Without Paragon and the Fairy Queen* locates the source of the king's power in that allegorical nature, that humanized cosmos, viewed as a human dimension, which inaugurated the garden as the place of all proportions, hence of all disproportions.

Hermann Pitz's *Waterdrops* are a mockery of form, an impasse of natural sculpture, the indeterminate mark of idea on matter. Pitz's water drop is at the limit of identification, classification; it eludes botanization, the calculated order of the garden. Dew would be more natural than the nature of the seventeenth century — it would reproduce the fiction of an origin, a new measure beyond any scale. These drops of water could restore the illusion of a frame, as enormous photographic lenses, a wonderland in which nature would lose its human reference.

## The Tableau, the Image, Outside the Frame

According to Virginia Woolf, the novel appeared as a fable plucked from the other world, in which the imagination was always referred to an indeterminable model: the cosmos. The reason for this was that until the eighteenth century, all "representability" was anchored in an imaginary sphere that was an authority for presentation. The world was figurable because, according to Alexander Gottlieb Baumgarten's *Poetics*, representation is a "heterocosmic fiction." Yet between the "station" defined by the king—the ideal viewpoint, a vanishing point, a reference to the infinity of the garden—and the "view," the formation of a frame for the sensibilities, there is a whole aesthetic order, which reverses itself, dividing into two, forever irreconcilable domains.

On the one hand, the spectator is the center of an either geometric or projective disposition; on the other hand, the frame becomes a preliminary form, a schematism that arranges the world in a tableau. "The image of the destroyed object and the very deconstruction of the image are not dissociable. Preserved, conserved, rendered museographic, the image also has at stake the destruction of the order of representations from which it surges."[9] The image becomes a surface for the sensibilities, a thought in tableau form of the Kantian critique that allows the formation of the world in the order of the system of knowledge.

It is such a temporalization of painting for a subject that Marin Kasimir (*Garden View—the Waterfall—Courtyard View*) breaks from a conflagration of the structures of representation. The stage is a mirror, an allegory of a fountain; the tiers are a mountain; the garden benches are made of cutouts from an image, from painting. The physical time of the frame image is methodically cut out, and then reordered in architecture; the nature of the theatergarden then seems like an assemblage of qualitatively different times, of orders that in no way correspond to one another. The reversibility of forms escapes or defies the discourses on representation—illusory deconstructions produced by the same essence that they expose. The image leaves the frame, offering itself in a simultaneity that distinguishes neither subject nor object; the view becomes the structure of vision; each person forms an order to his own measure.

As Walter Benjamin showed, the ideology of vision is inseparably tied to its technological and social structure. When Roland Barthes wrote a text on the Eiffel Tower, demonstrating that the tower is the suspension of the gaze over the totality of

Paris, his overall view still fit in with this status of the frame image.[10] Thus, breaking through the frame would turn every object of representation into a new picture.

"Theatergarden Bestiarium" permits the viewer to transcend all discourses on a possible deconstruction of illusionism and images. The Bauhaus, as Dan Graham has written, failed in its effort to "control" the image, since it always took it for granted as the term or referential identity of representation. Yet the contemporary games with simulation seem prey to the same contradiction. The mimicking of the postures of a critique of illusionism—sculpture-painting, mockery of the object, Jean Baudrillard's simulacrum, the "systematization of the unessential," as he wrote in 1968 (*The System of Objects*)—remains within the frame; it is merely the overexposure of the image that leaves the frame empty. Bernard Tschumi's cinematic experiments, the sequences that are supposed to constitute the park, the garden of follies in La Villette, still link the stage and the inscription. Forming the image outside the doubling of a determination of the frame means giving in to the internal duplicity of "mimesis," which establishes "the frame as a paragon, which both constitutes it and batters it, which makes it both hold out and collapse." One must therefore think of the image in the determination structure of the frame; "the deconstruction must never reframe nor dream of the pure and simple absence of the frame; these two apparently contradictory gestures are the systematically contradictory gestures of that which is deconstructed here."[11] The resolution of the frame opens up the sole possibility of an interrogation of the juridical unity of the artwork—a question about its autonomy, its value, the judgment that can be pronounced upon it. The formation of this gaze without distance seems to be the object of Fortuyn/O'Brien's piece (*Scala*). Made entirely of plexiglass, the construction encloses an interior, an intimate space, that it does not close up. The metalwork motif defines the opening—an opening upon a transparency in which light becomes the sole material element. The tiers, the steps of the theater, are nothing but a motif or idea, the lines of a terracing, a gradation of the procedures in architecture; in their axis, the tissue, the curtain of light, define nothing; one has to leave the point of view, circle around the piece in order to establish the stage, in order to see the work materialize in a frame that is directly realized by the spectator—as the very definition of the image.

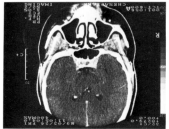 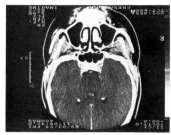 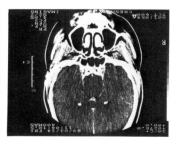

*X-rays of human skull.*

## The Sole Singularity

"Theatergarden Bestiarium" is a gathering. Rüdiger Schöttle wanted to conceive of the whole as a community of works in which the social and economic constraint forces a withdrawal to one's own work, a huddling over an increasingly contorted identity, a narcissism that each artist would like to hurl in the face of the world. Where is the unity—of a knowledge, of a history, of an ethics—that would still allow us to establish divisions, to judge, to classify, to put in order? That which we used to be able to call a relativism has been transformed into a vast network of exchange, in which performance—social, economic, strategic—is the only thing that makes for a hierarchy. Cynicism is a value, like morality, if it is operational in a context; it is no longer a position of retreat, an individual attitude. Then what about the work of art? Is it capable of working out, all by itself, its stance—art against craft, against the industrial product, against the image . . . or must it join forces with them?

"Theatergarden Bestiarium" proposes a logic of presentation that blurs the line between public and private, in which the identification breaks down before the totality, in which the desire (an aesthetic desire) to totalize collides with the disparate plasticity of the works. "Theatergarden Bestiarium" offers no spectacle; rather, it suggests a wandering—the uncalculated time of a stroll in which each work transcends its objective state, imposing an accomplishment upon the spectator, an internal liaison that gives him measure, his unity.

"Theatergarden Bestiarium" restores to each work of art of which it is composed an autonomy that the work seems to have lost on the stage of international exchanges. Where the contemporary artist is now maintained or supported by an economy of dispossession, renunciation of property, playing with signs of universal recognition on the surface of a glaciation of all personal implication, it becomes urgent to restate the question of the autonomy of the aesthetic sphere. The point is not to reaffirm an identity, or set up new criteria, or establish a new ethics. It is more important to specify that this so-called "objective" art actually survives in the shadow of a monstrous economy of that which is one's own, an economy of identity—directly escaping from the most oppressive part of the nineteenth century. This surface art, this market art, which claims to be critical because it bares the way the institution functions, never problematizes the ontological unity of the work. "Theatergarden Bestiarium" seizes the right of register, taking us before a visual plurality that has to be determined at every moment, because it escapes the continuum of being "publicized."

"Theatergarden Bestiarium" is placeless; it is gnawed at by the public space. "Theatergarden Bestiarium" is utterly disincarnate. It respects no unity of proportion; not even the psycho-geography of the Situationists can give it a coherence. "Theatergarden Bestiarium" is the tragic flip side of our desires for objectivation; it forces us to give each element its dimension, its quality in the philosophical sense, a singularity that opposes appropriations.

This essay has been excerpted from a text commissioned by The Institute entitled *Without a Paragon and the Fairy Queen: The Stage and the Register.*

[1]Jean-Marie Apostolides, "Fêtes dans les Jardins de Versailles sous Louis XIV," in *Traverses,* nos. 5 and 6 (Paris: Editions du C.C.I., 1976), p. 87.

[2]The festivals of the enchanted isle in Versailles during 1664 borrrowed the plot of a tale by Jean de Prehac, "Sans Paragon" ("Without a Paragon"), *Conte moins contes que les autres. Sans paragon et la reine des fées* [*Tale Less of a Tale Than the Others. Without a Paragon and the Fairy Queen*] (Paris, 1698).

[3]Werner Oeschlin, "The Theater of Invention," *Lotus International* (Milan), no. 17 (1977): p. 71.

[4]Richard Sennett, *The Tyrannies of Intimacy,* French translation, p. 88.

[5]Quoted by Denise and Jean-Pierre Le Dantec in *Le Roman des Jardins de France* [*The Romance of the Gardens of France*] (Paris: Editions Plon, 1987), p. 110.

[6]I am referring to Jean-Luc Nancy's *Le Partage des Voix* [*The Separation of the Voices*]. Here, according to Jacques Derrida, the author develops a radical critique of the inscription, as a substitute for the letter, the voice (*Stimmung*). *Stimmung* is a German word meaning "mood"; *Stimme* is a German word meaning "voice." This accord is also a "fateful division of logos itself," according to the conception of "difference" developed by Derrida. See Jean-Luc Nancy, *Le Partage des Voix* (Paris: Editions Galile, 1982), p. 82.

[7]Ludger Gerdes takes up the idea of a materialization of the artwork, which, according to Theodor Adorno, rejects all purism as a regression to traditional idealism. Beyond the dialectical concept of the image, in which the recourse to temporality remains debatable, Gerdes reevaluates the notion of the ornament as the establishment of an "image" in direct correspondence with the social paradigms of representation and expression. See Ludger Gerdes, "Einige Bemerkungen" ["A Few Remarks"], *Kunstforum International* (Cologne) 65 (1983): pp. 80–81.

[8]Elie Konigson, "Scène, décor, illusion" ["Stage, Décor, Illusion"], *Ligeia,* no. 2 (1988).

[9]Henry-Pierre Jeudy, *Parodies de l'auto-Destruction* [*Parodies of Self-Destruction*] (Paris: Librairie des Meridiens, 1985), p. 76. The author, developing a semiological analysis of social

systems, radicalizes a notion of "frame image," which reinforces its structure by being drained of its content. This line of thinking is very close to the concept of interface developed by Paul Virilio.

[10]Roland Barthes, *La tour Eiffel* [*The Eiffel Tower*] (Paris: Delpire, 1975).

[11]This ability of the frame to juridically define the unity of the artwork reveals why all the contemporary aesthetic strategies have carefully avoided this issue of law, the entire historical field in which the signature impulse is pursued. No "theory," no "practice," no "theoretical practice" can interfere in this area if it does not weigh on the frame—a decisive structure of the stake, ultimately invisible to the inwardness of the senses, "sheltered by the entire hermeneutist, semiotist, phenomenologist, and formalist traditions—and all the empiricism of the extrinsic." See Jacques Derrida, *La Verité en peinture* [*Truth in Painting*] (Paris: Champs Flammarion, 1978), pp. 71 and 85.

*X-ray of human skull.*

76

*Grotto of Orpheus, Hellbrunn, near
Salzburg, 1613–19.*

# THE THEATER IN THE GARDEN

## FROM ARTIFICE TO ARTIFACT

*Naomi Miller*

*The satirical scenes are to represent Satire, wherein you must place all those things that bee rude and rusticall . . . for which cause Vitruvius speaking of Scenes, saith they should be made with Trees, Rootes, Herbs, Hils and Flowers, and with some country houses, as you see them here set downe. And so that in our dayes these things were made in Winter, when there were fewe greene Trees, Herbs, and Flowers to be found; then you must make these things of Silke, which will be more commendable than the naturale things themselves.*
Serlio, The Book of Architecture[1]

PROLOGUE: TRADITION OF THE PASTORAL IN THE SIXTEENTH CENTURY
Rooted in antiquity, the pastoral found its ideal milieu in the gardens of Renaissance courts. Theatrical presentations revived the dreams of Arcadia set down by Vergil, Ovid, and Theocritus, as contemporary poets composed their bucolic odes in imitation of the ancients. Pastoral dramas such as Giovanni Battista Guarini's *Pastor Fido* and Torquato Tasso's *Aminta* were perfectly suited to the rustic mode.

Artifice enhanced the décor when Alfonso II d'Este of Ferrara had an island erected for the production of *Aminta* in 1573. While elements of the actual landscape were transported to the stage, the garden itself became the *mise en scène* for a wide variety of theatrical presentations. Villas and chateaux harbored natural scenery that could be manipulated to serve as theaters, with trees, shrubs, and hedges providing natural backdrops and forming the wings of the stage. Such natural components were further enhanced by perspective designs producing illusions of extended or contracted space, suitable to the geometric layout of the garden.

Not surprisingly, the penchant for garden theaters had its beginnings in the art of sixteenth-century Italy, which created a dialogue between nature and art. That theater and garden had long since been wed is visible in Donato d'Agnolo Bramante's design for the Belvedere Court of the Vatican palace and in the garden of the Villa Giulia, where the focus of the central axis is the terminus formed by the sunken hemispheric nymphaeum—in antiquity, a fountain house—set against a classical scenic background. Spectacles on a grand scale took place in the amphitheater of the Boboli Gardens. Built in the seventeenth century on the site of a Renaissance garden theater, the horseshoe-shaped arena rose in stone tiers along the hillside. Marble statues designed in the style of the antique, together with terra-cotta urns, were highly visible against the lush verdure. Opposite, the garden façade of the Pitti Palace

Jean Le Pautre, the king's festivities at Versailles, July 18, 1668.

Antonio Lafreri, Courtyard of the Vatican Belvedere by Bramante, Rome, 1565.

*Israel Silvestre, first day of the king's festivities, Versailles, May 7, 1664. The procession of the king and his chevaliers.*

*Israel Silvestre, first day of the king's festivities, Versailles, May 7, 1664. The banquet of the king and the queen.*

*Israel Silvestre, second day of the king's festivities, Versailles, May 8, 1664. Performance of* Princesse d'Elide *by Molière.*

with its imposing fountain formed an appropriate grandstand for observing tournaments, processions, and theatrical presentations.

Renaissance theorists, in accord with the treatise of Vitruvius, created stage scenery in imitation of nature as a proper background for satyric scenes and pastorals. At the same time, the garden itself, whether set in town or country, became the natural locus for all manner of court ceremony and entertainment. Its very layout exploited new discoveries in perspective and optics and thereby introduced hitherto unexplored spatial dimensions, while fountains and grottoes functioned as scenographic elements.

Versailles is the paradigmatic theatrical palace and garden, its wonders a source of fascination to later European monarchs and master builders. Between the grandeur of these royal gardens, ultimately derived from the experiments of the Italian Renaissance, and the gardens of the Enlightenment, lies the German eighteenth-century Baroque garden. In its assimilation of currents north and south of the Alps, the latter may be used as a barometer to demonstrate the transformation of the geometrically designed Renaissance garden to the sentimentally dominated Romantic garden of a later era.

### THE GARDEN AS THEATER: VERSAILLES

No gardens are as theatrical as those of Louis XIV's Versailles, and no royal court was more preoccupied with the quotidian as theater. Little wonder that only the gardens and park could provide a stage sufficiently vast to accompany the most magnificent displays of pomp and pageantry. *Les Plaisirs de l'Isle Enchantée, ou les Fêtes et Divertissements du Roy, à Versailles* allow us to witness the magic transformation of the garden in a series of performances, ballets, banquets, mock naval battles, and fireworks designed to produce a total work of art. Based on Lodovico Ariosto's *Orlando Furioso*, the program began on May 7, 1664, and ended three days later. Israel Silvestre's engravings have preserved these festivities, beginning with the procession of the king, his chevaliers, and their retinue about the ring course, in the guise of Roger and other knights imprisoned on the enchanted island of Alcina. Apollo is seated on a triumphal chariot, with allegorical figures of the four ages. The stage setting for this celebration is an architecturally disposed amphitheater, defined by hedges with trees rising above, parting for a central clearing on the principal avenue to the palace. Later in the day, the Four Seasons appeared, as musicians strummed on their instruments and courtesans and shepherds, bearing lavish gifts and sumptuously laden platters, recited verses before the king and queen.

In Silvestre's engraving of this scene, three simulated pedimented porticoes composed of verdure are arranged symmetrically, the middle one flanked on each side by arched doorways for entries and exits. On the second day, the same *allée* was transformed by a rectangular frame, embellished with shields and trophies, which acted as the proscenium arch — in reality, the open-air path of the garden, wherein a comedy by Molière and the *Ballet de la Princesse d'Elide* were performed. The theater for the third day included a ballet on the island of Alcina, whose Enchanted Palace rises on a rocky mound. Screens, held down by ropes attached to blocks at the pond's edge, were painted with pastoral landscapes appropriate for their role as stage wings. The last and most spectacular engraving of the series depicts the destruction of the palace within a blaze of dazzling pyrotechnics, and with it, the delights of the island of Alcina.

Festivities in the park of Versailles on July 18, 1668, are also recorded in engravings. Concerts and banquets were set within green cabinets, whose arbors opened upon nymphaea and gardens, creating an organic architecture of diverse flora and fauna. Jean Le Pautre's engravings for these spectacles show an awesome mélange of fire and water on the canal at Versailles — the vibrations crackling above the triangular structures crowned with mythological figures and a central obelisk surmounted by a radiating orb. Nocturnal illumination delineates the palace midst pyramids, fountains, and classical sculpture, concluding the account on the sixth day. However, divertissements and extravaganzas only accentuated the daily round at Versailles, where every facet of court life was part of an elaborate ceremony. As the theater incorporated the garden, so, too, the gardens were transformed into theaters. Not a bosquet or basin, fountain or grotto, labyrinth or walk, *allée* or parterre was without its scenic components. Witness, for example, the actual Water Theater, begun in 1671 under the architect François d'Orbay; its fountain display was a hydraulic marvel. Few waterworks could rival the seemingly infinite combinations of gravity-defying jets of water repeating their wondrous cycles.

That all of the garden could be converted to theater is perhaps most evident in the Grotto of Thetis, which, in the words of André Félibien, was "a place where Art works alone, and that Nature seems to have abandoned." In 1674, this ultimate allegorical artifice to glorify the Sun King provided the setting for a presentation of Molière's *Le Malade Imaginaire*. However, an extraordinary inversion of art and nature occurred a century later (1778–81), when the marble protagonists of the grotto, Apollo and his attendant nymphs, were transferred to the newly designed stage, set within a rocky promontory in a garden grove.

*Jean Cotelle, Water Theater, Versailles, begun in 1671 by François d'Orbay.*

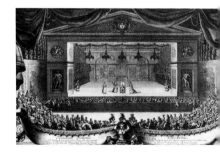

*Jean Le Pautre, the king's festivities, performance of* Le Malade Imaginaire *by Molière in front of the Grotto of Thetis, Versailles, 1674.*

*Hubert Robert,* The Baths of Apollo in Versailles, *1778–81.*

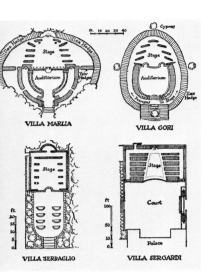

*Sheldon Cheney, comparative plans of sixteenth-century Italian garden theaters.*

*Peter Schenk,* A General Prospect of the Royal House and Garden at Herrenhausen, *near Hanover, engraving, 1720.*

## THE ARBOREAL THEATER:
### FROM THE *TEATRO DI VERDURA* TO HERRENHAUSEN

Alfresco theaters were particularly suitable to the proliferation of the pastorale in the second half of the sixteenth century, providing an idyllic locale for the nymphs and shepherds who recreated an Arcadian world. Could a more perfect setting be imagined than the *Teatro di Verdura*, with its retaining wall and auditorium engulfed by clipped hedges and the natural greenery of the park? By conveying a heightened sense of intimacy, this small, verdant enclosure was particularly appropriate for the aesthetic of princely courts and private estates.

Sheldon Cheney has analyzed the components of sixteenth-century Italian garden theaters. In his comparative study of the genre at the villas of Marlia just outside Lucca, and Gori, Serraglio, and Sergardi near Siena, we are struck by the almost equal areas occupied by the stage and auditorium. Not only do these plans reinforce the immediacy of court productions, but they also elicit the possibility of audience participation, most ideally in the masque, in which the actor and the audience join in the dance at the conclusion of the performance. Unlike architectural theaters, the stage depth of the garden theater is greater than the width, decreasing toward the rear. Usually of green turf or gravel, the stage floor is raised three or four feet above the auditorium. Seats were arranged before the performance, though we note that the Serraglio theater is equipped with stone seats, emphasizing its relatively miniature proportions. At Sergardi, the palace courtyard functions as the auditorium, thereby allowing the garden façade's windows to be used as box seats. Cypress, yew, or ilex hedges, often enhanced by elaborate topiary or *broderie* work, formed the wings onstage as well as the boundaries of the entire theater. Variations are ever present. At the Villa Garzoni (formerly Collodi) at Pescia, the stage is carved into the hill, with the auditorium delineated by a widening of the garden path. Large masses of cypress walls and screens for wings characterize the stage at the Villa Marlia, the whole surrounded by overhanging trees. The clipped box hedge of the prompter's enclosure marks the front of the platform, and a low hedge masks the "lights" used for evening performances. Edith Wharton's description of the theater at Gori gives a vivid portrait of the type:

*Another antique alley of pleached ilexes, as densely shaded but not quite as long, runs from the end of the terrace to a small open-air theater which is the greatest curiosity of the Villa de' Gori. The pit of this theater is a semicircular opening, bounded by a low wall or seat, which is backed by a high ilex-hedge. The parterre is laid out in an elaborate* broderie *of turf and gravel, above which the stage is raised about three feet. The pit and the stage are enclosed in a double hedge of ilex, so that the actors may reach the wings without being seen by the audience; but the stage-setting consists of rows of clipped cypresses, each advancing a few feet beyond the one before it, so that they form a perspective running up to the back of the stage, and terminated by the tall shaft of a single cypress which towers high into the blue in the exact center of the background. No mere description of its plan can convey the charm of this exquisite little theater, approached through the mysterious dusk of the long pleached alley, and lying in sunshine and silence under its roof of blue sky, in its walls of unchanging verdure. Imagination must people the stage with the sylvan figures of the* Aminta *or the* Pastor Fido, *and must place on the encircling seats a company of* nobil donne *in pearls and satin, with their cavaliers in the black Spanish habit and falling lace collar . . .; and the remembrance of this leafy stage will lend new life to the reading of Italian pastorals.*[2]

The auditorium of the Hedge Theater at Herrenhausen, 1750, built by Martin Charbonnier, 1689–92.

Baroque gardens perpetuated the species. Composed largely of topiary works—geometrically contrived hedges in the form of pyramids, cones, cubes, ovoids, spirals, and spheres—they created a luxurious background of verdure for the pageantry of the contemporary theater. An earthly paradise seemed within reach of the splendidly accoutered spectators who promenaded midst sparkling plays of water and antique props in all their gilded glory. Nature constituted the walls of this verdant theater; clipped hedges of box, lime, hornbeam, and yew planted in rigid lines formed the stage and wings, while a curved hedge often served as the amphitheater for the audience.

Among the best-preserved hedge theaters is that in the garden of Duke Ernst Johann Friedrick at Herrenhausen, the summer palace of the electors of Hanover, designed by the French landscape architect Charbonnier. Built from 1689 to 1692, its survival is tied to descendant Elector George Louis's ascension to the English throne as George I in 1714. Almost lost in the maze of geometric parterres in the garden, the hedge theater is the natural counterpart of the architectural palace theater. Concave, stepped terraces shape different levels of the stage, whose center is marked by a receding series of hemicycles. Between the theater and the auditorium is a wide path that was probably occupied by the orchestra. Seats of the auditorium are arranged in diminishing one-point perspective, a central aisle lined by statues on both sides and flanked by eleven rows of hedge flats, the geometry of the theater contrasting with the picturesque landscape of the park.

*The stage of the Hedge Theater at Herrenhausen, 1751, built by Martin Charbonnier, 1689–92.*

Sometimes theaters utilized already extant garden structures. Just before the steps ascending to the Temple of Apollo at Schwetzingen—a garden complex often likened to Versailles—lies a garden theater situated within a grove (1762–76). Musicians occupied the lower space, while spectators were seated on adjacent terraces between statues of sphinxes and reclining water nymphs.

THE STONE THEATER AS RUIN:

FROM HELLBRUNN TO THE HERMITAGE TO SANSPAREIL

Perhaps the oldest open-air theater in northern Europe is found in the garden at Hellbrunn, designed for the archbishop of Salzburg, Marcus Sitticus von Hohenems. Hollowed out of natural rock situated within a wooded hill, the theater, built in 1617, was formed of a semicircular apse with provisions for scenery and hangings and props; carved grottoes on either side probably served as spaces for the orchestra and dressing rooms. In the words of Johann Bernhard Fischer von Erlach:

*Nature has been the only architect here and has even exceeded what art could have done. . . . Continuity of the view requires, likewise, no other ornament than what nature has given it, to render it fit and convenient for stage plays, which have been frequently presented upon it. The reverberation of the sounds among the rocks is extraordinary.*

Imagine the court listening to Claudio Monteverdi's recently composed *Orfeo* under the arch of this imposing rock-cut theater!

Here, too, in the castle at Hellbrunn was the Grotto of Orpheus, who is depicted playing his lyre, with Eurydice at his feet, within a stalactitic arch. Even more dramatic was a Roman Theater (1613–19), whose stone seats were pitched in accord with the horseshoe-shaped amphitheater. Its accessories included a table and stools with playful automatons and water jets to set diners reeling midst statuary of Roman emperors and gods. Surely, the author of these grotto theaters had recourse to the hydraulic wonders disseminated by the treatises of Salomon and Isaac de Caus, based upon the works of ancient scientists and mathematicians.

Relatively rare, the stone theater conceived as a ruin introduces a new principle in mid-eighteenth-century garden theaters. Whereas the open-air garden theater or hedge theater—with its stage wings fanning out in fleeting perspective— parallels the vistas of Renaissance gardens, the ruin theater aims to reawaken the spirit of antiquity. Unbound by archaeological precedents, such as the reconstruc-

*Fisher Von Erlach, Rock Theater, Hellbrunn, near Salzburg, 1721.*

tion of the ancient Roman theater, the ruin theater, like the cabinet of curiosities within the palace, is more akin to a museum piece placed in the garden; it is primarily a monument, replete with historical and literary associations. Occasionally used for performances and festivities, the ruin theater may be considered among the classical topoi of eighteenth-century English gardens, the most notable of which are the Egyptian pyramid, the cave of St. Augustine, the temple of Bacchus, the grotto of a river god, the hermit's lodge, the Gothic tower, the tomb of Vergil, and shrines to the virtues and to concord and liberty.

This compendium of classical and medieval revivals was nurtured by landscapes after the antique, largely transmitted by the ancient authors. Antiquity extended to the ineffable state of nature as well as to its stones and walls overgrown with creeping moss and weeds, which simulated a melancholy atmosphere of decay and death. In the attempt to revive and understand the ancient theater by means of archaeological reconstructions, landscape architects found it sufficient to build the Roman theater as a ruin.

One of the earliest known ruin theaters is that of the Hermitage, near Bayreuth, constructed in 1743–46 by Joseph Saint-Pierre. Among a series of fanciful edifices, which included rusticated pavilions, grottoes, aviaries, an orangery, and a hermitage, the theater was conceived as an artificial ruin. Ordered by the Margravine Sophie Wilhelmine, a sister of Frederick the Great and daughter of the elector of Brandenburg, Frederick William I, king of Prussia, it was erected to accommodate open-air performances of court musicals, operas, pastorals, and plays.

The plan of this ancient theater constructed as a ruin contains a sunken green lawn; eight steps connecting the lawn and turf; a grassy slope on a different level between flights of steps; a raised, sand-covered field where the audience was to sit; and the steps. There was no masonry amphitheater, nor was the main element of the ancient theater, the cavea (auditorium), present. The stage, sixty-eight meters high and seventy-nine meters wide, is six meters seven centimeters above the ground of the parterre (pit, stalls, and orchestra); arches, springing from the vaults from five pairs of ashlar piers, span the stage. Two engaged columns mark the proscenium arch, bearing the entablature of the Doric order. Tendrils of vines and weeds and corroded stone niches add to the appearance of desolation and disintegration. While still incomplete in 1744, the theater was the stage for the performance of an Italian opera with ballet and a French comedy, on the occasion of the marriage of the margravine's sister. Despite the theater's unfinished state, the temporary décor

*Temple of Apollo, Schwetzingen, near Heidelberg, built by Nicolas de Pigage, 1762–66.*

included intricately hung colored lamps, a portrait of the bride accompanied by casts of sea gods, and a bust of the goddess Fortuna on the foreground arch. The after-theater supper was held in the amphitheater, with the diners seated in a gigantic shell.

The Margravine Sophie Wilhelmine's pretensions to the intellectual life, beginning with her French education and continuing with a lifelong nurturing of the arts, were exploited in the rock garden at Sanspareil, near Zernitz (1745–48). The site of the park was a rocky glade, similar to a petrified island, which prompted the margravine to base the program of the garden on Fénelon's *The Adventures of Telemachus* (1699). As in the contemporary English gardens of Hoare at Stourhead and Shenstone at the Leasowes, the margravine conceived of the landscape as an epic poem. Here she reenacted the narrative of the *Odyssey* in grottoes of Calypso and Diana and Vulcan. In the Calypso Grotto, a natural rock formation, composed of stone, tufa, and pebble mosaic, serves as the proscenium arch of the ruin theater. Aspects of wilderness alternate with remains of antiquity, telling of the wanderings of Ulysses and his return to Ithaca. Four pier columns carry the rustic stone arches spanning the stage, while the rear is closed by two low-arched portals of similar character on either side of the proscenium. Ideal relief portraits of Homer and Vergil in oval medallions are hung on the side columns; beneath them are statues of seated satyrs. Keystones of the arches are further adorned with a bust of Medusa and a tragic mask, while Hermes, Terminus, and masks of fauns are sculpted on the rear wall.

The third arch is fragmented as befits a ruin; hence, the stage partakes of the same desolate character as that of the Hermitage, simultaneously elegant and rude. Serving as the auditorium, the Grotto of Calypso, situated under a vaulted stone arch, completes the illusion. Traces remain of the multicolored stones and shells that once adorned the stone columns. In the words of a nineteenth-century observer, it seemed as if "this theater grew from the earth."[3] The lower stage is a closed orchestra space in front, with connecting flights of steps on both sides. Stone wings join the flat plan of the stage with the parterre.

Erich Bachmann has noted the dual significance of the Sanspareil theater as Romantic/ironic and moralistic.[4] Theater and artistic ruin, stage wings and decorative material, belong to different categories of reality—the wings to the illusionistic aspect of the theater, the ruin décor to its moralizing sentiment. By overturning the fictive world, the ruin becomes reflective of the transitory nature of life and the vanity of all earthly things.

*Chaveau, stage design by Giacomo Torelli for* Andromède *by Corneille, 1650.*

## Epilogue:
### Toward the Romantic Era

As the play attempts to fix intangible ideas, to give substance to past reality, the ruin theater by its very existence stands as a countercurrent. Unlike the theater, which is governed by the illusion of reality, the ruin as an emblem of the eighteenth-century garden transports us to an imaginary or remote sphere. Whether recalling the past of antiquity or the Middle Ages, its purpose is to evoke a state of meditation attuned to melancholy or unnatural solitude. Ruins are metaphors for death and dissolution and hence symbolize the transcience of worldly matter.

Whereas the hedge theater imposed an order on Renaissance villa gardens, prompted Louis XIV to subjugate nature to his control, and spurred the revival of the Augustan Age in gardens of the Enlightenment, the ruin theater is emblematic of another animus. It is related to those garden structures that resurrected a classical pilgrimage, one distinct from the archaeological reconstruction of ancient theaters as envisioned by Renaissance architects and humanists. The mergence of the ruin with the garden foreshadows the Romantic Age. Partaking of a natural cycle of bloom and decay, the ruin becomes an end in itself, a picturesque setting of transitory splendor. It is nature that bears the sign of antiquity, of nostalgia and the passage of time, and, not least, of memory. "In the ruin, history has physically merged into the setting. And in this guise history does not assume the form of the process of an eternal life so much as that of irresistible decay." Thus Walter Benjamin's exploration of Baroque allegory recalls the vicissitudes of the garden theater in time and place.[5] Gardens and theaters harbor the potential to transport us to realms beyond our ordinary experience. The ruin theater provides an escape to the distant past and at the same time gives us a glimpse of man's limits of understanding. Meditating on times long gone, we are inextricably confronted with our destiny.

[1]Sebastiano Serlio, *The Book of Architecture* (1611; reprinted, New York: Benjamin Blom, 1970), II, iii, 1545, fol. 26.

[2]Edith Wharton, *Italian Villas and Their Gardens* (London: John Lane, 1904), pp. 72–75.

[3]Rudolf Meyer, *Hecken-und Gartentheater in Deutschland im XVII. und XVIII. Jahrhundert* (Emsdetten, 1934), p. 230.

[4]Erich Bachmann, *Felsengarten Sanspareil* (Munich: Bayerische Verwaltund der Staatlichen Schlosser, Garten un Seen, 1979), p. 50.

[5]Walter Benjamin, *The Origin of the German Tragic Drama*, trans. John Osborn (London: NLB, 1977), pp. 177–78.

*Koppel, Prologue of* Andromède *by Corneille at the Calypso Grotto, proscenium of the Ruin Theater at Sanspareil, near Bayreuth.*

*Koppel, Ruin Theater in the garden of Sanspareil, near Bayreuth, 1745–48.*

*Ruin Theater at the Hermitage near Bayreuth, built by Joseph Saint-Pierre, 1743–46.*

Office for Metropolitan Architecture (OMA), drawing for Parc de Villette Competition, 1982–83.

# GARDEN AS THEATER AS MUSEUM

*Dan Graham*

*The site was empty. . . . There was to be an enormous amount of educational gardens, of scientific gardens, research gardens, exotic gardens; there had to be gardens in which the surrounding neighborhood could indulge in some of the most modern media of the twenty-first century. . . . There was a cybernetic dimension; there were corporate gardens.*
*Rem Koolhaas on the Parc de la Villette competition[1]*

*Renaissance gardens and villa in Merate, Italy, seventeenth century.*

The first Italian Renaissance gardens, built astride Roman ruins on hillsides, were sculpture gardens, theaters, archaeological museums, alfresco botanical encyclopedias, educational academies, and amusement parks that drew on special effects to entertain the public. Their meaning was either moral or allegorical, natural or scientific, and political lessons were incorporated into their designs.

As "art forms" they were models of a world intended to be studied. Archaeological excavations, including local statues and sculpture from far away, were exhibited *in situ* when they related in theme or period to a particular garden. These spaces contained botanical collections, minerals, and other natural curiosities. In Florence's Orti Farnesiani, classical sculpture was displayed in juxtaposition to every plant mentioned in classical literature.

The Renaissance garden symbolized the Edenic, pre-Fall of Christian man and of Arcadian (Roman) time that was associated with earthly paradise, a mythical past, or a future utopian time of eternal pleasure and natural harmony. Through its Arcadian associations with paradise, the garden embodied all that was pleasure and a contrast to man's worldly existence. The garden transported him to another world: *. . . in which everything laughs and is full of love, of joy, and of wonder, and where the flowers and herbs not only delight the corporeal eye of the beholder, but by very subtle means pass into their minds.[2]*

The designs of Renaissance gardens were often derived from classical texts. One of the most influential texts was Ovid's *Metamorphoses.* In his poem, Ovid brings together the natural and the artificial in a metamorphic chain in which nature imitates art, and conversely, in which the artificial mimes the natural. The Boboli Gardens in Florence, a triple grotto whose architecture appears to yield to "natural" rock decorating the outer edge of the grotto and descending around its entrance, is a fine example. Its "natural" effect was artifice escalated to almost Disney-like proportions, creating a childish fairyland:

*James Mason, A View in Vergil's Grove, at the Leasowes, designed by William Shenstone, near Birmingham, 1748.*

*Falda, Nymphaeum, Villa Giulia, Rome, 1550s.*

*By the time we reach the entrance and see inside, our experience is a transformation of architecture into its natural materials; or, such is the ambiguity, of an opposite metamorphosis—rock and stone gradually shaping themselves into artifact. Inside this first room, this ambiguous world is heightened by a scenery of man and animals who are either emerging out of, or changing into, stone.[3]*

Gardens contained various allegorical memory places. Artificial memory in the Renaissance was an attempt to resurrect what originally was a part of Greek, and later, Roman, rhetoric. In order to memorize long sequences of speech in a culture without readily available written texts, a metaphoric chain of ideas was symbolically associated with specific architectural places. One sign might be imagined to be in the forecourt, the next in the atrium; others were associated with statues. Each symbolic space, in relation to other signs and architectural symbols in the garden, was designed to trigger certain memory responses in the visitors.

So one would not be confused with another, distinct intervals separated each memory space. Imagistically striking loci prevailed in gardens: grottoes, statues, and inscriptions. Each image stimulated a specific idea or theme. The garden as a whole could be viewed as a theater in which one strolled from one stage to another, from scene to scene, and in so doing, reactivated certain memories and allegorical images within the environment.

Guilio Camillo's Teatro del Mundo was the ultimate model for the garden as a memory theater. It attempted to create an association between memory and symbolic images. These images were magic, talismatic representations of a coded system of the world. Camillo's encyclopedic memory machine—no one is clear as to whether it actually existed as a transportable pavilion or an unrealized idea—was intended to exist as an actual miniature theater large enough for one spectator-scholar, who could stand in the central stage area. The spectator was to use the device to learn the structure of the universe from microcosm to macrocosm, as in a modern science museum's representation of subatomic physics or outer space.

Camillo reversed the conventions of spectator to stage; the audience member was to be on the stage, instead of looking at the spectacle on stage. Each tier in the Teatro del Mundo represents aspects of the "universe expanding from First Causes through the stage of creation." Images of planetary gods were placed on the outside of each tier. Under these images were "boxes containing masses of papers, and on these papers were speeches, based on the works of Cicero, relating to the

*Giulio Camillo, Memory Theater, mid-sixteenth century.*

subjects recalled by the images." Teatro del Mundo's ultimate goal was not to "expose reality, but to reveal a hidden one through a different scheme." This scheme was embedded in the architecture. The structure's ultimate purpose was like a Jesuit exercise: to remake memory. Memory was given the coherence and micromacrocosmic meaning denied in ordinary life.

A typical Renaissance garden was first viewed and entered from a loggia at the base of a villa. The garden's overall geometric plan was seen as if in a perspective painting or from the back of a theater looking straight at the stage. The apse was like a stage's proscenium overlooking the garden below and prepared the visitor for later closeup views of the garden's statues, flora, vistas, and emblematic narrative flow.

By the period of the Italian Baroque, garden design and theater design were so closely connected that they directly influenced each other. The Baroque garden, treated metaphorically as a vast, natural theater, usually contained one or more areas for theater performances. The theater's architectural boundaries were defined by boxed hedges, grass, stones, statuary, and fountains that also formed the staging and seating areas. The sets of such productions sometimes utilized the garden's actual pathways, radiating in perspective through the garden, or they represented the garden's perspectives as part of the temporary set designs.

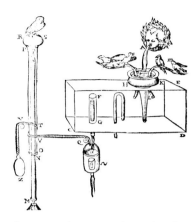

*Singing Bird Fountain, located in the water garden of the Villa d'Este at Tivoli, near Rome, 1550–80, after the original invention by Heron of Alexandria.*

### THE ENGLISH GARDEN

The English landscape garden of the early eighteenth century continued the Italian tradition of the garden as an outdoor theater of moral allegory. One of William Kent's earliest garden designs, Chiswick, begun in 1731, extended the garden plan into a virtual replica of Andrea Palladio and Vincenzo Scamozzi's Teatro Olimpico, whose five streets disappeared in perspective into an urban plaza. The Teatro Olimpico was the model for Renaissance stage designs that replicated the surrounding cityscape. In Chiswick, instead of urban streets there were grass lanes that terminated in buildings and obelisks, emphasizing the unresolved relationship between urban and rural.

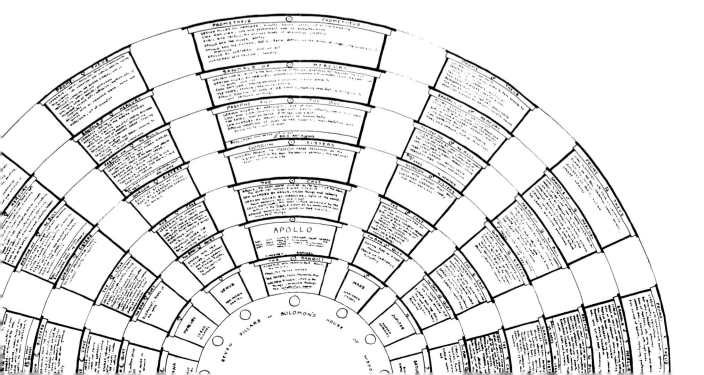

The Elysian Fields section of the garden at Stowe, constructed in England between 1720 and 1740, was a liberal Whig allegory against the restored British monarchy. Designed by William Kent and Charles Bridgeman for Lord Cobham, Stowe translated to garden plan an essay by Joseph Addison from *The Tatler*, which presented a "dream" in which the walker experienced the human condition by passing through a garden whose paths provide insight into human and political motivations. Approaching "middle age" the dreamer walked on a straight road with laurels, behind which were trophies, statues of statesmen, heroes, philosophers, and poets. This path led to a Temple of Virtue, which hid a Temple of Honor behind it. Visible through the arch of the Temple of Honor was a crumbling structure, the Temple of Modern Virtue.

Addison's "dream" was translated into the "constructed" ruin, a Temple of Modern Virtue, built as a ruin seen from the future,[4] yet looking back to the past. It dramatized the corruption of the present, monarchist regime. A headless statue of then Prime Minister Robert Walpole stood next to the ruins. Across the River Styx stood the Temple of British Worthies, with busts of a Whig Hall of Fame in semicircular niches around the forum. They included Francis Bacon, John Milton, William Shakespeare, Elizabeth I, Inigo Jones, and Alexander Pope, among others.

### THE FRENCH "ENGLISH GARDEN"

The English garden, transplanted to France, became a "garden of sensibility" in which an elegiac view of death was represented by an Arcadian garden. When death was encountered, it was in a "peaceful setting fraught with sweet melancholy and nostalgia." Various monuments evoked Arcadia as a pastoral retreat and as a sublime memorial evoking "those tender feelings of which we are susceptible when we revive the memory of a lost friend."[5]

In 1730, Alexander Pope built his English garden around a memorial shrine to his mother. Pope's example was extended by other garden builders, and a cult of burial memorials to dear or noble friends, especially to those who had visited the particular garden, sprung up.

Ermenonville, designed by the marquis de Girardin, was inspired by Jean-Jacques Rousseau's writings. The garden translated philosophic categories into their emotional evocation in specific picturesque pavilions, arrangements of the natural landscape, and various recreations, including bucolic villages with working farms,

*Rocque, plan of gardens at Chiswick, Middlesex, England, 1753.*

*Donnowell, Patte-d'Oie at Chiswick, Middlesex, England, 1753.*

peasant villagers, and meadows. The Temple of Philosophy was built as a ruin. Left in an unfinished state, it signified:

*. . . the imperfection of human knowledge. . . . Dedicated to Montaigne, the former monument is the occasion to evoke the Philosophers and their contribution to humanity: Newton—light, Descartes—the absence of void in nature, Voltaire—the ridiculous, Montesquieu—justice, Penn—humanity, Rousseau—nature.*[6]

*Bickham the Younger, Temple of Modern Virtue at Stowe, Buckinghamshire, 1750.*

*Jacques Rigaud,* View of the Queen's Theater from the Rotunda, *Stowe, Buckinghamshire, England, 1733.*

Rousseau's "cottage" was a hermitage. Hermitages in English gardens in France were somewhere between primitive huts and pseudomedieval "ruins" and supposedly constructed for homeless, wandering monks, philosophers, or the garden's owner, who might wish to detach himself from the cares of urban life. Rousseau's dwelling had a view of a lake, and beyond it, of an Arcadian meadow containing a medieval village and tower. It was modeled after descriptions in his own *La Nouvelle Héloïse.* Rousseau died and was buried at Ermenonville, his tomb designed by the painter of archaeological ruins and architect of artificially constructed ruins, Hubert Robert. Rousseau's tomb on the Isle of Poplars, along with the Altar of Reverie, which marked the place where the writer often stopped to rest, evoked an Arcadian, sentimental mood in which the dead thinker's life was remembered.

The natural change of seasons, water, and rocks were used to symbolize feelings of fear, tranquility, sorrow, or the sublime. Rock formations provoked astonishment, vexation, and terror. The forest, by its elevation and expanse, was meant to be considered in heroic terms. Peaceful, solitary, serene, melancholic scenes were designed according to the layout of the trees. Water was sublime; it ran deep.

By the mid-nineteenth century, with Baron Georges Haussmann's plan for Paris's redesign, central parts of the city were transformed into English gardens, traversed by spacious, tree-lined boulevards. The overt rationale for these urban, sylvan spaces was to bring "airy greenery and light into crowded districts."[7] Their unstated purpose was to mask the boulevard's political and military functions.

Boulevards facilitated communication between various city districts and allowed the military easy access to any point in a city. They also countered a rebellious proletarian's tactic of "taking to the streets." Haussmann's reorganization of Paris involved the creation of a politically defensible capital city whose arteries were accessible at all times by troops and made for rapid communication between parts of the city and the central government.

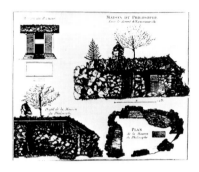

*Laborde,* Village of Ermenonville, *designed by René Louis Girardin, 1766–76.*

*Moreau le Jeune, Jean-Jacques Rousseau's first tomb on the Poplar Island, Ermenonville, 1778.*

*Plan of the philosopher's hut, overlooking the large lake at Ermenonville, 1778.*

The city's new, open boulevards with civic squares and plazas were also used by rulers from Napoleon onward to turn Paris into an outdoor museum. The city was to become an exhibition space designed for the education of the emerging middle class, a "collection of permanent reminders" of the historical greatness and hegemony of, not only "the French nation, but also of the comparable—though slightly lesser—contribution of mostly subservient Europe."[8] This idea is perhaps the first appearance of a recurrent nineteenth-century theme:

*the city as a museum . . . a positive concert of flirtations with the Saracenic remains of Sicily . . . culture and education . . . as benevolent course of random but carefully selected information. . . . The city as museum mediated . . . classical decorum . . . [with] the . . . liberal impulse . . . and free trade.*[9]

### THE BIRTH OF THE MODERN MUSEUM

The bourgeois, national museum as an educational institution developed simultaneously with the capital city as an outdoor museum. It was meant to foster a new nationalism separate from classical Greece or Rome, or even the Italian Renaissance tradition. "Recognizing French Gothic as one of the most daring conceptions of the human spirit," the national museum was to be an aid "toward happiness in being French." Ideas of didacticism and moral improvement for a new middle-class notion of public education emerged as a national priority and, as such, helped to justify a "national" collection:

*A museum should be instituted according to two points of view, one political, the other concerned with public instruction from the political point of view. It should be established with enough splendor and magnificence to speak to every eye. . . . From the instructional point of view, it should include everything the arts or sciences could together offer to public education.*[10]

The Abbé Alexandre Lenoir, chief propagandist for the national museum, originally housed his collection in the church of an abandoned convent. This proto-French national collection, organized between 1796 and 1800, divided French cultural history into epochs, with one hundred years as the basic time unit. Each room or century was given the "character, the exact physiognomy of the century it should represent." Fragments of surviving windows, doors, and other interior décor were added to the surface of the room's walls to give authenticity.

Anthony Vidler, the Anglo-American architectural historian, remarked that "in each of these rooms, despite Lenoir's frequent protestations that everything

*Merigot,* The Arcadian Prairie, *Ermenonville, 1776, designed by René Louis Girardin.*

has been executed according to notes taken from the actual monuments of the time and after the proper authorities," his theatrical virtuosity generally overcame his historical accuracy. As Vidler admitted, "the whole shows the effects that can be produced in decoration with old details skillfully applied."

*Alexandre Lenoir, Musée des Monuments Français, fourteenth-century gallery, 1816.*

### Winter Garden and Garden Cities

At the same time as Haussmann was politically rationalizing the street plan of Paris to bring militia as well as hygienic air and greenery into formerly overcrowded, polluted environs, artificial streets, or *passages,* were being built in Paris for shoppers. These glass-roofed shopping arcades were devoted to the display of commodities. They created phantasmagoric "dreamlands" of product display. The mercantile display devices of arcades, new department stores, and trade fairs culminated in the Paris Universal Exposition in 1889. For Walter Benjamin, the German social historian and art and literary critic, these glassed-in settings were a "dream world . . . in which individual consciousness sinks into ever-deeper sleep . . . [and] generates hallucinations or dream-images."[11] Benjamin saw commodities creating a dream of ever-newness, in which each new product causes the spectator to forget the now devalued, passé commodity, idea, or fashion.

The same artificial "dream" was induced by the winter garden, which allowed exotic and tropical vegetation to be displayed even in the temperate or cold climates of northern, industrial, urban European cities year-round. The winter garden, like the shopping arcade and Sir Joseph Paxton's Crystal Palace at the International Exhibition in London in 1851, were replicas of a world within a world. With the appearance of the winter garden, the meditative, private garden was replaced by the public botanical garden-museum and became a place for mass education and entertainment and a temporary refuge from everyday life.

Utopian, garden-city settlements were proposed throughout the nineteenth century as a way of employing technology to create a more ideal structure as a socialist, bucolic antidote to the capitalistic city. Such ideal communities were to be located outside a city in self-sufficient garden settings. Instead of individual houses, extended families would share work and child-rearing responsibilities to create an economically and socially efficient "machine for living." The efforts of nineteenth-century reformers influenced the later commercial development of suburban garden towns around 1900.

After the First and Second World Wars, suburban settlements were located

*The Place de l'Etoile, designed by Georges Haussmann. From 1853 to 1870 Haussmann worked on the transformation of Paris.*

*The raising of the Obelisk Luxor, Place de la Concorde, Paris, 1836.*

*A showcase at the Philadelphia Centennial Exhibition, 1876.*

on the edge of a city's boundary, adjacent to and resembling those first picturesque park cemeteries whose design had evolved from the elegiac Elysian Fields of the English garden's monuments to the dead. Like cemeteries, suburbia's "garden" evoked a nostalgic sense of perpetual peace in its well-manicured shrubs and green lawns. Accommodating working-class families in their own suburban homes helped to stabilize and defuse the revolutionary potential of the inner-city working class. With the growth of a more stable, lower middle class, small nuclear family suburbs helped create a new consumer society based on home consumption.

### BIRTH OF THE AMUSEMENT PARK

For the working class left in the city, the birth of electric lighting made possible new types of leisure, nighttime consumption. Projected light filled previously dark spaces, providing an illusory world of personal pleasure and "dream." Electric lighting was responsible for both the birth of film and of the amusement park. It was around 1900 that Freud's notion of the "unconscious," the cinema, and Coney Island simultaneously appeared.

Rem Koolhaas, the Dutch architect, discusses the development of Coney Island as an unconscious dreamland in the midst of the waking, rational world of New York City in his book *Delirious New York*. Coney Island's first amusement complex, Luna Park, which opened in 1906, followed nearly the same scenario and dreamlike, science-fiction fantasy of Georges Méliès's film *A Trip to the Moon* (1902). A visitor entered the park's lunar landscape in much the same way an astronaut begins a trip to the moon:

*The ship is 1,000 feet in the air. A wonderful, wide-eyed panorama of the surrounding sea, Manhattan, and Long Island seems to be receding as the ship mounts upward. . . . The moon grows larger. Passing over the lunar satellite, the barren and dissolute nature of its surface is seen. The airship gently settles . . . and the passengers enter the cool caverns of the moon.*[12]

Luna Park's neighbor was Dreamland, built around an inlet of the Atlantic Ocean. Its entrance porches were underneath huge plaster-of-Paris ships under full sail; metaphorically, the surface of the entire park was under water.[13]

Other simulations in Dreamland were the midget city of Lilliputia, in which "the midgets . . . have their own Parliament, their own beach complete with midget lifeguard and a miniature . . . Fire Department responding to a false

*The Fresh Water Aquarium at the World Exhibition in Paris, 1876.*

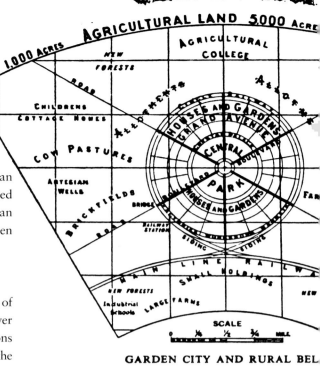

GARDEN CITY AND RURAL BELT

Ebeneezer Howard, diagram of the
Garden City and Rural Belt, 1898.

alarm"[14]; a simulated ride in a submarine; an enactment of the fall of Pompeii; an Incubator Building in which premature babies from the area were actually collected and nursed to health in technologically advanced facilities; a ride on Venetian canals; and a set that fabricated a New York City block where each night firemen demonstrated how to fight the flames of a burning building.

### THE CITY TO THE SUBURBS

The spread of suburbia after World War II correlated with automobile's alteration of American life. The new middle-class, suburban family was more transient than ever before, more willing to pack up and move quickly to another location. Corporations spread and decentralized, shifting their staffs from branch to branch throughout the country. This suburban, automotive period also saw the rise of drive-in cinemas and shopping malls. It was the use of the automobile for leisure and the decline of the urban cinema that led to the many highway theme parks, of which Disneyland is the best known example.

Like the nineteenth-century trade exposition, the theme park became a spectacle of capitalist ideology. Disneyland's Tomorrowland had, until recently, housed General Electric's New York World Fair *Carousel of Progress*. This was a film-and-slide dreamland that presented the idea of progress, or "better living" through commodity technology.

Visitors sat as if in a slide carousel, moving ahead in time incrementally in a circular progression, in which they experienced "progress" through a series of tableaux of a family of natural-looking robots in a middle-class kitchen. The sequence progressed in twenty-year segments, from the turn of the century onward. Between each section, the audience was encouraged to sing along with the robots: "It's a great big beautiful tomorrow, shining at the end of every day. Man has a dream and the dream can come true."

Each time the audience sang, the carousel magically advanced—the whole theater unit actually moved—twenty years onward, but the same family was in the same setting—almost. The robots were imperceptibly older, and their clothing and the décor had been changed to reflect the styles of the time. However, the most significant changes, which the family was always emphasizing, was the kitchen's electricity-based home technology. History was neutralized by the ever-new, by progress. The circular motion of the carousel expressed endless technological progress, endlessly satisfying human needs.

Hendon Garden Suburb demonstrates how the idea of uniting work, home, and nature were forgotten in the beginning of the twentieth century. Nature becomes ornamental.

Owen Jones, Palace of the People, London, 1859.

Log Flume—*a water ride featured at Six Flags Great Adventure, a chain of amusement parks across the United States.*

Louis Marin, French art historian, sees Disneyland as an allegorical narrative in which spectators as "actors" perform the text as entertainment. Disneyland is a cynical inversion of such early American utopias as those of the Shakers, the Mormons, and the Hudderites—as well as European communal socialist experiments proposed by Louis Fournier and Robert Owen that attempted a reconciliation of Rousseau's return to freedom and innocence of nature with urban technology's promise of liberating man from enslaving work. Disneyland, according to Marin, attempts to resolve central contradictions in the ideological myth of America:

*Disneyland is a . . . displaced metaphor of the system of representation and values unique to American society. This projection has the function of alienating the visitor by a distorted and fantasmatic representation of daily life, by a fascinating picture of the past and the future, of what is estranged and what is familiar. . . . In "performing" Disney's utopia, the visitor realizes the models and paradigms of the society in a mythical story by which he imagines his social community has been constructed.*[15]

Disneyland as a semantic map consists of a division into three places or concepts:

1.      The outer limit defined by the parking lot where the visitor leaves his car. As the car is one of the most powerful markers of his daily life, in leaving it behind and exchanging his behavior for a free field of consumption and play, the visitor enters the imaginary realm of The Magic Kingdom.

2.      The intermediate area where the visitor purchases tickets and Disneyland money in order to participate in Disneyland life.

3.      The visitor's actual entrance into Disneyland at the embankment of the Santa Fe and Disneyland Railway with its subsequent stations.

The railway leads to the park's central strip, Main Street USA, which separates Frontierland and Adventureland. As the route to Fantasyland, the railroad is the axis. Marin notes that in Adventureland and in Frontierland, Main Street USA represents America itself in present time:

*By selling of up-to-date commodity goods in the setting of a nineteenth-century street, between adult reality and the childish fantasy, Disney's utopia converts commodities into signification. Reciprocally, what is bought there are signs, but these signs are commodities. . . . Main Street USA signifies to the visitor that life is an endless exchange and constant consumption.*[16]

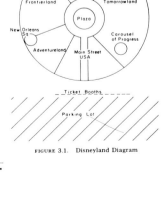
This cinematic version of American history as mythology is equivalent to the use of Ovid's *Metamorphoses* in the Renaissance. In Disneyland, Marin proposes, man is twice removed from nature:

*All that is living is an artifact. Nature is a simulacrum. Nature is a wild, primitive, savage world, but in this world is only the appearance taken on by the machine in the utopian play. In other words, what is signified by the left part of the map is the assumption that the Machine is the truth, the actuality of the living. . . . In Tomorrowland machines are everywhere: from the moon rocket to the atomic submarine. . . . [These machines] are scaled-down models of the actual machines. We have false duplicates of living, and concealed mechanistic springs on the left, obvious machines on the right.*[17]

On the left of a large, free-standing map are Adventureland and Frontierland. Adventureland with wildlife in exotic countries is viewed during a boat trip down a tropical rain-forest river. It defines America in relation to the savage outside world it has conquered, as opposed to Frontierland, which shows the American conquest of its own savage interior.

Both are imperialist myths. To the right of the map is the future, Tomorrowland, in opposition to the past of Adventureland and Frontierland. In Tomorrowland the universe has been conquered in the future by science and technology. America's ruling 1950s and 1960s imperialist mythology, progress, the mythology of the American corporation, prevails.

While the Italian Renaissance Baroque garden was based on a tension between the artificial and the natural, Marin suggests that in Disneyland nature itself is only a representation, the other side of which is a machine.

## The Corporate Atrium as Museum and Garden

In its interior atrium, "a rectangular hole inserted in a seventy-story cylindrical tower clad in reflecting glass," Atlanta's Peachtree Center Plaza Hotel (1976) is a typical John Portman building, a tropical resort in the center of the city. From the outside, the tower looks like a rocket in its gantry; it is connected to the building by bridges at each level. The floor of the tower is covered by a reflecting pool, or, as Jonathan Barnett, who collaborated with Portman on a book dealing with Portman's work, has written: a "half-acre lake . . . [in which] boat-shaped islands are pushed out between the columns, forming places to have a drink and observe the space and the people."[18]

*Louis Marin,* Disneyland: A Degenerate Utopia, *analytical diagram of Disneyland, and semantic structure of the ideological representation in Disneyland, 1977.*

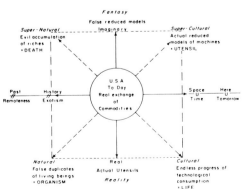

FIGURE 3.1. Disneyland Diagram

Semantic Structure of the Ideological Representation in Disneyland Utopia

*Emilio Ambasz, Lucille Halsell Conservatory, San Antonio, Texas, 1984. The conservatory is surrounded by sunken courtyards set in the rolling lawns of a botanic garden.*

**98**

Portman's hotels link the dreamworld of Luna Park and Disneyland to the recreational Arcadia of the picturesque city park. Landscaping techniques are brought indoors to create the mood of a film set.

The glass-topped Parisian arcades, the world expositions, and the European winter gardens of the nineteenth century were first adapted by the United States at the turn of the century, when they were used in hotels and in commercial office buildings.

The best-known corporate office building with a central glass skylight design was Frank Lloyd Wright's Larkin Building, built in Buffalo in 1904, but now destroyed. Employee and management desks were democratically arranged on balconies, stacked in tiers along the interior walls and in the central court. Each member of the corporate "family" could view each other in and through an open central court. Strong, overhead sunlight pored through the central skylight.

During the 1960s, the American city center came to be dominated by high-rise office buildings. But by the early 1970s, following the economic recession after the Vietnam War and the Nixon administration's cutbacks in funding for blighted, older, East Coast cities, the streets surrounding these corporate headquarter towers were threatened by crime. An initial solution was to build medieval fortresslike megastructures enclosed in concrete. Services, retailing of goods, and pedestrian traffic became concentrated in a protected, central court. Following the lead of Portman's hotels and Kevin Roche's Ford Foundation garden atrium design, the substitution of an atrium skylight and "ecological" greenery created an accessible pedestrian corporate office building lobby that was safe.

In the 1970s the atrium space became a way of competing with and paralleling the suburban shopping mall. As the upper middle class moved back to the city from the suburbs, the atrium was adapted to suburban forms. Real trees and earth were combined with high-tech features and suburban patiolike design. Green-and-white metal openwork chairs and green lettering on shop windows connoted a suburban Arcadia in the midst of a city—an urban fantasy of the picturesque brought into the central city.

New York's Chem Court, a glass-encased structure, alters its appearance with fluctuations in natural light. Inside the court of the bank building, anodized aluminum columns, water-filled canals, a tiered marble fountain, and stone-faced planters comprise a mini-botanical garden. The plants are oversized versions of domestic, suburban house plants, but they are labeled in the style of a botanical

*Whitney Museum, Equitable Center. Equitable Center by Edward Larrabee Barnes. Museums are increasingly dependent on corporations for financial support. By associating with "high culture," businesses enhance their public image.*

*IBM Atrium and entrance to the IBM Gallery of Science and Art, opened in 1983 IBM Building, Madison Avenue, by Edward Larrabee Barnes, New York.*

garden. Seasonally changing displays are maintained by the staff of New York's Botanical Garden. Labeling creates the civic-minded aspect of an educational garden and gives the impression—only partially accurate—that Chem Court's atrium is an extension of the New York Botanical Garden.

Corporate atriums and lobbies already function as part of the New York museum system. The Whitney Museum has three museum branches in corporate lobbies, while the IBM Corporation lobby contains its own botanical garden-style atrium and, below it, a separate underground museum. Battery Park City, a "public-private" financial center and highrise, high-income housing development, has created a new riverside park, open to the public, but maintained by private security. It also functions as an outdoor "art museum" in which artists such as Richard Artschwager, Scott Burton, and Siah Armajani have created "public amenities."

The solar-heated, high-tech space capsule, wedded to the nineteenth-century winter garden, defined the look of these mid–1970s corporate garden spaces. They can be considered a political allegory related to the Whig's political allegory in Stowe. The oil shortage and ecological crisis of the mid–1970s undermined the public's perception of the corporation's ideology of "better living through chemistry" and scientific progress. The corporate garden merges the 1960s space machine *2001: A Space Odyssey,* with the ecological, utopian dream of earth as a "garden," or suburban patio garden. Corporations were then able to deny the historical crisis, the ecological movement, and the movement's radical critique of the 1960s energy-wasting high technology.

## CITY AS HISTORICAL MUSEUM

While the 1970s saw the birth of the interior, corporate park-atrium, American cities were also creating new outdoor plazas that emphasized a continuity with the past. As part of the 1976 U.S. Bicentennial celebration, Washington and Philadelphia rebuilt their city centers, emphasizing historical reconstruction.

Washington is a city metaphorically visualized as a park, being partly based on the gardens of Versailles. Within its double network of orthogonal and radial roads of urban forest—nature made into an object of civic use—are fifteen public squares for the fifteen states of the Union.

Venturi, Rauch, and Scott Brown's 1978 plan for a new public square off Pennsylvania Avenue—a second, less complex plan was eventually executed—consisted in part of a two-dimensional map of Pierre Charles L'Enfant's original plan of the city, which was to be inscribed on a marble court, as well as scale models of the White House and Capitol buildings, and a replica of the Mall, which like the original, was to be simply flat glass. The plaza was to be read as a miniature scale model of the city, which, in the context of the actual city surrounding it, would juxtapose the original, historic, and ideal plan with the city's present reality. The map and the models would have aligned themselves to the local, rectilinear street grid. The idea was to accentuate the smaller scale's relation to the local neighborhood, the historic and tourist aspects of the city, and to restore the central axis of Pennsylvania Avenue.

The original plan was to have had two tall, thin pylons, which would have related to the present-day, overblown scale of Washington, a deviation from its original neoclassical plan. Seen from a distance, the pylons would have appeared monumental, "purposefully abstract and simple," like other monuments of Washington, but they also were meant to have been read as simple, linear framing devices.

The pylons, as abstract markers, were to appear to correct present-day Washington—reinstating the grid of the original plan—and then point to the nearby Treasury Building, blocking the intended clear view along Pennsylvania Avenue from the White House to the Capitol.[19] In a manner similar to William Kent's eighteenth-century plan for Chiswick, in which the *allées* were terminated by smaller-scale versions of famous English architectural monuments, Venturi wanted to terminate his smaller-scale map with the actual monuments of Washington.

However, the plan with the pylons was not accepted. Venturi, Rauch, and Scott Brown's realized plaza is a flat plane, three-and-a-half inches above the existing sidewalk. L'Enfant's plan is inscribed on its marble surface. The grassy mall is represented by real grass. Numerous quotations from important architects, city planners, presidents, and other public figures about Washington, D.C., have been inscribed on it. Streets are represented by black marble against white marble ground. The Basin and Reflecting Pool, between the Jefferson Memorial and the Washington Memorial, is of black marble etched with lines signifying "waves." The waves can be "felt" through people's feet, scaled up to be an abstract reduction of the actual street plan that surrounds it and that it represents. The linear marks are incised into the sign one walks on. One "feels" with one's walking body, as a blind person's hands "read" Braille. Venturi describes the plaza as picturesque.

*Venturi, Rauch and Scott Brown with George E. Patton, Inc., landscape architect, Western Plaza, at Pennsylvania Avenue, Washington, DC, 1977.*

### Parc de la Villette

Parc de la Villette, a science and cultural center, located at the northern margins of Paris, is surrounded by a traditional working-class neighborhood. La Villette was formerly the slaughterhouse district. It is bisected by motorways, working canals, and the edge of an industrial suburb.

The French Socialist government conceived the Parc de la Villette plan as part of a large-scale urban planning project intended to balance the growth of upper-income and corporate tower slabs, extending from the affluent western area of Paris, toward the center and south by creating an area that was to be educational and recreational. It was also meant as a counter to the highly popular Centre Georges Pompidou located in a fashionable center-city district.

Parc de la Villette consists of a Museum of Science and Technology, a music center, sports and recreational facilities, a performance center, day-care and community centers, and gardens. Remnants of La Villette's past—industrial archaeology—have been left standing and are integrated into the new plan: a gigantic nineteenth-century cast-iron market structure and an unfinished concrete slaughterhouse and meat market built in the 1960s.

Parc de la Villette was originally conceived as part of a planned—then canceled--1989 World's Fair. The program for the La Villette competition specified that the design seek a reconciliation:

*. . . between the natural environment and urban civilization and that it allow the local impoverished classes access to the twenty-first-century information as well as recreation, while attracting other Parisians and foreigners to the section. It should help in "rebalancing . . . Parisian development to the east."*[20]

La Villette attempts a merger of the 1968 Paris General Strike's "liberationalist" notion of pleasure with an attempt to broaden the French educational system to overcome a traditionalist, elitist approach to scientific knowledge. The program given to the architectural contestants outlined specific facilities for a park, as well as a desire to seek a solution that would theoretically question the role of the historical, anti-working-class urbanism found in Haussmann's parks. Specifically, La Villette would contain:

*educational facilities, such as a library; spaces for various kinds of exhibits, some permanent, such as an astronumerical garden comprising a radio telescope, an amateur observatory . . . workshops for production and creation, hosting group*

*Venturi, Rauch and Scott Brown, with George E. Patton, Inc., landscape architect, Western Plaza, at Pennsylvania Avenue, Washington, DC, replica of the Capitol (detail), 1977.*

*Philipp Thomas, François-Xavier Mousquet, and Thierry Louf, drawing for* Jardin de la Sequence 7, *Parc de la Villette, Paris, 1986.*

*music, photo, cinema, video, model making . . . microcomputers, gardening. Also sports facilities . . . play areas, thermal baths . . . social facilities . . . a diversity of eating places from sophisticated restaurants to . . . picnic . . . areas. Also a market and permanent shops [as well as] entertainment facilities, such as an outdoor theater and concert areas."[21]*

The park was to relate to the biology exhibits contained within the Museum of Science and Technology through outdoor thematic gardens that would exhibit plant growth with a goal to expose and inform, while avoiding any overly stated, didactic character. These gardens would include orchards, beehives, and botanical gardens, and incorporate a water garden, rose garden, mythical garden, scent garden, tinctorial plant garden, practical garden, wheat garden, fruit garden, weed garden, moss, fern garden, vegetable garden, and underground mushroom bed.[22]

In the competition, the scheme of OMA, the Dutch architectural firm headed by Rem Koolhaas and Stefano de Martino, was initially awarded first prize; then the verdict was reversed in favor of Bernard Tschumi's more practical scheme.

OMA's scheme used strips similar to a beach-front amusement area. When hybrid boundary conditions meet, the result was to contain, at the two respective boundaries, elements of both strips, but with their own unique aspects.

OMA's proposal acknowledged the specific location of the park, which Koolhaas called a "kind of suburban plankton."[23] A strip of sports activities might adjoin a strip of tropical gardens, which, in turn, might adjoin a swimming pool and a strip of theaters. Superimposed on this series of strips would be a pointlike grid. These points were not meant to define an activity, but be permanent architectural elements such as kiosks, theorems, greenhouses, and play areas.

Tschumi's plan, also formed from an overlay of different systems on a grid, contains pavilions or follies placed on a point-grid system at 120-meter intervals. Each folly is a $10 \times 10 \times 10$-meter geometrically deformed cube. This system of follies is, in turn, superimposed on a linear route, such as:

*The Path of Thematic Gardens . . . a random curvilinear route that links various parts of the gardens . . . providing unexpected encounters with unusual . . . or "programmed" nature.[24]*

Another group of coordinates are surfaces, which "receive all activities

*Cedric Price, Fun Palace, footbridge, climbing frames, and exhibition hall, 1965.*

requiring large expanses of horizontal space for play, games, body exercise, mass entertainment." Tschumi likens the linear route to a cinema device, such as an unrolled filmstrip.[25]

In their emphasis on user-determined pleasure and learning experiences, as well as in their use of overlapping grids to provide a fragmented, multi-use service environment, both the Tschumi and Koolhaas schemes recall 1960s Archigram and proto-Archigram work of Cedric Price, the English architect and theorist.

Price's Fun Palace, designed between 1962–67, was meant to be a flexible, indeterminate leisure environment, a "serviceable environment in which visitors could choose from and participate in varied activities, not a conventional architectural building."[26]

Price believed that "leisure facilities must be used by society as an active social-sensing tool, not merely a static predictable service."[27] Fun Palace was to have been an amusement arcade, a music space where instruments could be borrowed for spontaneous jam sessions, a science playground with learning activities, a closed-circuit television area, and a meditation space. In the plan, a giant space frame incorporates fifteen latticed steel towers, each contained at the top by tracks to carry movable cranes with equipment to various parts of the site. The supporting towers were to contain not only services, but architectural elements—ramps, walls, floors—all movable and interchangeable. Specific environments were to last no more than a few hours or days.

The Tschumi and the OMA proposals differed in how their plans acknowledged the physical and historic context of the Parc de la Villette's site and in how their plans related to a predetermined topology of the park.

Tschumi's professed strategy was to negate the surrounding context as well as the just-past notion of "park" or "world's fair":

*La Villette is anti-contextual. It has no relation to its surroundings. Its plan subverts the very notion of border on which "content" depends. . . . For today the term "park" has lost its meaning. . . . La Villette . . . aims at an architecture that means nothing. Its plan subverts even the very notion of borders on which context depends.*[28]

OMA's plan, by contrast, acknowledged the suburban nature of the site and its surrounding border of intersecting mass highways. Movements along the highway were to give the auto passenger a quick series of changes and experiences. The auto ride preview would correspond to the ideal perspective the spectator had of the prospect of the

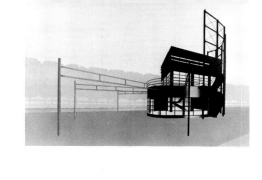

Bernard Tschumi, drawing of Follie J 7, Parc de la Villette, Paris, 1985.

Italian Renaissance park from the crest of the hill. The experience of approaching the park by car connects OMA's narrative strategy with that of the highway theme park.

Tschumi's follies, many of which have been completed, are designed both by Tschumi and by "guest" architects, philosophers, literary figures, and artists. Rather than denying historical precedent, Tschumi's notion revives the idea of the marquis de Girardin, who dedicated pavilions and scenographic areas of his park at Ermenonville to great men of philosophy, letters, and art. In Tschumi's plan, these great figures designed their own monuments, and the architect orchestrated and directed the ensemble. The selection of artists to work in teams with architects is a recent trend in corporate public art, as seen in the development of New York's Battery City Park, in which architects and landscape architects collaborated in plaza and park design.

The relation of the OMA scheme to the history of the landscape is twofold. It acknowledges the park as an allegorical, macro-microcosmic, utopian "Theater of the World," in analogical opposition to what is contemporary and debased in the day-to-day city. It connects the Renaissance park to Coney Island and the twentieth-century world's fairs in which science became emblematic of the future of humankind. Whereas the 1939 New York World's Fair's symbolic center was the Perisphere, which contained within its interior a scale model of the city of the future as depicted by modernist architects and planners, OMA's plan would make La Geode a mirrored sphere whose interior suggests a space capsule and whose panoramic film projections usually depict voyages through outer space in modern spaceships. The spherical form of La Geode derives from the archetypal modern world's fair spherical pavilions, which express the ideas that the cosmos and our earth are one world. The world's fair megasphere is an emblem of a promised future to be achieved through scientific progress that would unite us into one global community.

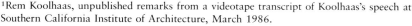

[1] Rem Koolhaas, unpublished remarks from a videotape transcript of Koolhaas's speech at Southern California Institute of Architecture, March 1986.

[2] John Raymond, quoted by John Dixon Hunt in *Garden and Grove* (Princeton, New Jersey: Princeton University Press, 1986), p. 6.

[3] Taegio Bartolommeo, *La Villa* (published in Milan in 1559), translated and quoted by Margaretta J. Darnall and Mark S. Weill in "Il Sacro Bosco di Bomarzo," *Journal of Garden History* 1, no. 1 (1984): 8.

[4] John Raymond, quoted by Hunt in *Garden and Grove*, p. 92.

[5] Quintilliam, "De Institutionee Oratoria," quoted by Frances A. Yates in *The Art of Memory* (Penguin, 1966), pp. 37–38.

[6] Frances A. Yates *The Art of Memory*, p. 141.

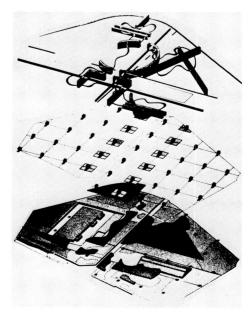

Bernard Tschumi, plan for Parc de la Villette, depicting the three architectural layers of lines, points, and surfaces, 1982.

104

7John Macky, "Journey Through England, 1724," quoted by John Dixon Hunt, op. cit., p. 197.

8Richard, A. Etlin, *The Architecture of Death* (Cambridge, Massachusetts: The MIT Press, 1984), p. 189.

9Joseph Heeley, quoted by Richard Etlin, op. cit., p. 176.

10Caisse Nationale des Monuments Historiques et des Sites, *Jardins en France, 1760–1820,* p. 77.

11Ibid., p. 59.

12Richard A. Etlin, "Landscapes of Eternity," *Oppositions* 8, p. 18.

13Ibid., p. 19.

14Ibid.

15Louis Marin, *Disneyland: A Degenerate Utopia,* Glyph I (Baltimore, Maryland: Johns Hopkins University Press, 1977).

16Ibid.

17Ibid.

18John Portman and Jonathan Barnett, *The Architect as Developer* (New York: McGraw-Hill Book Company, 1976).

19Robert Venturi, "Learning the Right Lesson from the Beaux-Arts," *Architectural Design* 49, no. 1 (1979): 31.

20François Barre, "Aux Portes du Parc," *L'Invention du Parc, International Competition 1982–1983,* Graphite Editions, 1984.

21Ibid.

22Françoise Choay, "Critique," *The Princeton Journal of Architecture: Landscape* 2 (1984): 212.

23Rem Koolhaas and Stefano de Martino, in *OMA Projects 1978–1981* (London: Architectural Association, 1981), p. 33.

24Bernard Tschumi, "Parc de la Villette," "Architectural Design," and "Deconstruction in Architecture," *Profile '72,* 1988.

25Ibid.

26Cedric Price, "Fun Palace, Camden, London," *Architectural Design,* November 1965, p. 522.

27Price, quoted in Jim Burns, *Arthopods,* Academy Editions, 1972, p. 58.

28Koolhaas, unpublished remarks from transcript of videotape, March 1986.

Norman Bel Geddes, General Motors Futurama, New York World's Fair, 1939, offering a vision of what America might look like in 1960.

Claude-Nicolas Ledoux, House of the Grounds Keeper, Maupertuis, France, 1785.

Marc-Antoine Laugier, The Personification of Architecture and the Primitive Hut, 1755.

# ARCHITECTURE THAT "SPEAKS"

## BUILDINGS FOR DISPLAY AND RITUAL

*Antje von Graevenitz*

Chinese students erect a replica of the Statue of Liberty, called "The Goddess of Democracy," Tiananmen Square, Beijing, May 1989.

Miss Liberty in New York Harbor represents more than an allegory of freedom. As a tower the Statue of Liberty is also a symbol for the "chosen." Following the tortuous path through the statue's interior, climbing the steps up to her head, one experiences her body as a symbol of individualization. It is not enough to look at this goddess of freedom and reflect on the freedom America stands for. One must also *act* in order to experience one's personal freedom. In this sense, Miss Liberty is both allegory, in its sculptural form, and ritual architecture, in its towerlike form.

Buildings that are less artistically significant can also possess a metaphysical meaning. Henry David Thoreau's hut at Walden Pond gave him shelter, but at the same time it served as a metaphor of the ego, a ritual location for reflection. Similarly, while the Rococo palaces of the eighteenth century in Europe were increasingly decorated in more festive and luxurious ways, their counterpart, the cottage, gained both an ornamental and a figurative meaning: it symbolized "nature as master builder," to quote a contemporary, the abbot Marc-Antoine Laugier, in his 1753 "Essay on Architecture." In these emotionally charged surroundings, the eighteenth-century lovers, the aristocrat and his partner, could strike the pose of innocents when, dressed as shepherd and shepherdess, they sought shelter for their love in the simple, albeit imitation, hut. They withdrew into nature, where the rules were different from those in the refined surroundings of the palace, the preeminent example of human power.

Palace and hut have a dialectical relationship: not only can a temple or a church have a metaphysical meaning, but so can a simple hut, provided the context assigns it this role and provided its creator is able to transmit his idea to the public. If his building does not do the job on its own, the architect can strengthen its meaning by, for example, attaching an explanatory plaque to the façade. He can also add features that have special significance, such as a cross or a Winged Victory. A builder can use figurative elements to give his structure a metaphorical meaning. By removing parts of a building from their traditional architectural context and transferring them to a new structure, the architect produces a building that resembles something it is not. A prime example is the appropriation of the façade of an ancient Greek temple for the front of a theater, or a bank, or a museum. The old façade lives on, but with a different interpretation. The architect can also place the building in a special site, the context of which provides another meaning. A park, a plaza, a world's fair, or even a city can extend the original intent of a building.

The general principle of symbolic architecture is that there is always more

*Frédéric Auguste Bartholdi*, Liberty Enlightening the World, 1883.

*Sainte Chapelle, the Chapel of the Kings of France, Paris, 1243–48.*

to it than meets the eye. The architect Claude-Nicolas Ledoux (1736–1806), who witnessed the French Revolution, even called his designs *architecture parlante* ("talking architecture"). Of course, architecture talks about as much as nature does; but signs are embodied in it that stimulate fantasy, intuition, and the power of association. In this way, the meaning of architecture becomes a fertile field of study.

One of the first art historians, the German philosopher Friedrich Schlegel, argued in his book *Grundzuege der gotischen Baukunst (Outlines of Gothic Architecture)*, written in 1804–1805, that the cathedral is a microcosm that reflects the eternal structure of Heaven. The United Nations building in New York City is a secular example of the same principle. The unity of all participating countries is reflected in the flags that ring the building and in the multitude of ornaments covering the interior walls. The United Nations was conceived as a utopia in stone. It is not yet a utopia, although people who work in the building are struggling to achieve that goal. The building reflects both practical and idealistic functions.

Around the turn of the century many architects dreamed of building a temple symbolizing the unity of mankind. Frank Lloyd Wright was the only one to realize this dream, expressed in his 1904 Oak Park Unity Temple near Chicago. For others the dream remained elusive. One of the best examples is the Pantheon der Menschheit (Pantheon of Mankind) by Dutch architect H.P. Berlage, designed in 1915. Berlage intended to glorify both the past and the present by representing the heroic deeds of mankind as statues, which the visitor would pass on his way through the long halls. The building had virtually no practical applications—the "holy mission" was all that counted.

Young German architects, suffering from a dearth of commissions after World War I, developed, under the name Glaeserne Kette (Glass Chain), designs for temples on mountaintops, devoted to eternity or to silence. They did not shun pathos. In their publication *Fruehlicht* (meaning "early light"—a reference to the new world born in the early morning sunlight), the architects of the movement, among them Bruno and Max Taut, expressed their belief in the idea of the "Holy House." The group waxed poetic about their aspirations: "The building is a picture of, and a salute by, the stars." Bruno Taut, who drew the floor plan of this imaginary building in the shape of a star, was also concerned with its "usage." He believed that the temple and its satellites should be reached only by airplane. Behind the airport, the visitor would be able to settle down immediately at one of the hotels, bars, or restaurants included in the plan. Beyond the service area, the visitor would find

himself inside the circle of the *Gesamtkunstwerk*, where the "children, preachers, and artists" lived in the three corners of a triangle whose points touched the circle's rim. The triangle enclosed the star-shaped house, the temple. All other areas in the circle would serve either practical or metaphysical purposes. Some buildings would be dedicated to love or to birth and death; others would be playgrounds or even factories.

The finished plan resembled a utopia, an ideal city. It also contained elements borrowed from the anthroposophical community founded by Rudolf Steiner at Dornach, a village near Basel, Switzerland. In 1913 Steiner had built, with the aid of his followers, the Goetheanum—a complex of buildings including a temple, a theater, and a university—on top of a hill. The center was shaped like an ovum in the state of division. It was a metaphysical metaphor, representing the spirit of a man-centered, rather than a God-centered, community, as a new beginning of life. The floor plan of the first temple, which burned down in 1922, resembles a skull; undoubtedly, the Goetheanum was meant to symbolize the brain of anthroposophy. The center was surrounded by residences in the same style, shaped like growing, organic forms, and by workshops with metaphorical exteriors. The most striking among these buildings, the one housing the boiler, has two "flames" made of concrete shooting into the sky.

Dornach was conceived as the beginning of utopia, an idea molded into architectural shape. Temples like these are displays in stone or wood of a permanent process of change, of the metamorphosis experienced by the visitor, the user, or the inhabitant of the building. They contain an educational message that only becomes intelligible when one understands the concept of buildings that are linked by ideas.

Metaphorical buildings often have a significant, even holy meaning. However, they also fit comfortably into gardens and world's fairs. Both Italian gardens, like the Mannerist park at Bomarzo, and English gardens of the eighteenth century were carefully crafted Elysian fields, where the visitor could amble along a *via sacra*, lined with oddly shaped or amusing buildings. At the famous Stourhead Park, in Wiltshire, England, the contemporary visitor is treated to a grand tour through the park, full of surprising buildings. He begins the tour at Stourhead House, dating from 1725, a fairly innocuous starting-off point. Shortly along the path, however, he is confronted with an obelisk, the ancient Egyptian sign for sun ray—the finger of the sun—symbolizing power and fertility. The obelisk is a signal that the visit is no ordinary one.

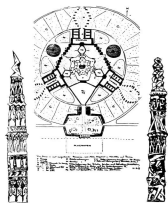

*Bruno Taut,* Airport, Column of Prayers *(left), and* Column of Sorrows *(right), in the magazine* Fruhlicht (Morning Light), *1920.*

*Rudolf Steiner,* Heizhaus (Central Heating), *Dornach near Basel, Switzerland, 1913–20.*

*Rudolf Steiner, Atelier Glashaus (Studio Glass House), Dornach near Basel, Switzerland, 1913–20.*

*Wallace K. Harrison, United Nations Building, New York, 1950.*

*Rudolf Steiner, First Goetheanum, Dornach near Basel, Switzerland, 1913-20.*

**110**

Henry Flitcroft, Temple of Apollo, *1765*.

*Stourhead Park, Wiltshire, England.*
*Henry Hoare I built Stourhead House in*
*the 1720s. His son, Henry Hoare II,*
*returned from his grand tour in 1741*
*and set about creating the landscape*
*garden with its architectural motifs.*

After pausing to admire the finger of the sun—or rather, the finger pointing toward the sun—the visitor continues on his journey by crossing a Palladian bridge. Bridges are the preeminent symbol of transition. As early as the Middle Ages the bridge had several connotations. As the boundary of a city, it was a legal symbol; as a customs station at the border, it was an economic symbol; as a place for communicating, it was a folkloristic symbol. Because processions frequently crossed the bridge, it also had religious connotations. In a similar way, the bridge at Stourhead, seen in the context of the other buildings in the park, is more than just a bridge. Only by crossing it can the visitor reach the Temple of Flora (built in 1745), the goddess of blossoms, where he can give thanks to the goddess for nature and its flowers through meditation. The visitor himself becomes part of nature. In the grotto (1748), which lies ahead on the walk, he can metaphorically experience his rebirth. The hermit's cell (1785), next to the grotto, instills in him the belief that human growth depends in large part on silence, wisdom, and solitude. Only when he has come this far in the tour is the visitor ready for the Pantheon, which commemorates the heroes of mankind. Of course, the real goal is to become a hero oneself. By climbing Alfred's Tower (1770), the visitor conquers his weakness of body and soul, a victory that rewards him with a magnificent view.

However, the journey is not complete. The visitor must cross another bridge (dating from 1860), made of iron, to reach—literally and figuratively—the Temple of Apollo. After crossing the bridge, the visitor passes a cascade (1766), where he can meditate on the watering of the earth, and a stone arch, which repeats the theme of regeneration. At the Temple of Apollo (the god of the sun, reason, and music) the visitor can contemplate the warming powers of the sun, the pleasure of order, the sound of music (in the eighteenth century, sounds were considered the composition of the world), and the importance of reason. But what is reason without the mercy of God? The Bristol Cross, dating from the fourteenth century and transported to Stourhead in 1765, reminds the visitor of God's grace. After transversing Stourhead's *via sacra*, the visitor is "initiated" into the rites of St. Peter's Church, which reminds him that even life after the Apocalypse will end on a positive note.

Buildings like Stourhead's, erected in parks and gardens, are often called follies: funny houses without any practical uses. But are they really useless? Their ideological context reveals educational ideas that unite classical and Christian cultural images. It is remarkable that educational symbols are used at world's fairs. After all, the avowed purpose of world's fairs—showing and stimulating competi-

Grotto, 1748.

The River God, 1748.

tion among nations in trade, technology, science, and culture—is completely opposed to notions of self-education.

Competition was indeed the main goal of the first world's fairs in the nineteenth century. The entire plan of the fair site was designed with this purpose in mind. The various countries exhibited their industrial and cultural products side by side. Orangeries seemed to have the ideal shape for these impressive displays, because they are virtually transparent and because they can be interpreted as a metaphor of the growth process of products. The most famous orangery of them all, Sir Joseph Paxton's Crystal Palace of 1851 in London, was widely praised for its functionalism and its restrained beauty.

Gradually, however, architects designed completely different buildings to convey a completely different message. In the world's fairs of 1834 and 1844 in London, the huge exhibition halls could be reached only by way of a bridge flanked by obelisks, the very symbol of the power of nations and of the sun, whose rays make products grow.

The 1867 Paris World's Fair was the first to have a consistent concept with its theme, "The History of the Earth." Visitors crossed a bridge to reach the fairgrounds, a symbolic transition to a place where they could have a once-in-a-lifetime experience. The exhibition was laid out in an elliptical form—had the architects been thinking of an egg?—with an oval-shaped park at the center. The schematic plan was not surprising, considering that the theme of the exhibition was "earth" as a closed unit. Alexandre Gustave Eiffel, a young architect who had been an assistant of master builder J.B. Sebastian Krantz at the 1867 World's Fair, designed for the next Paris fair, twenty-two years later, the famous Eiffel Tower. The structure not only provided visitors with a grand view of the exhibition, but it also gave a feeling of "rising above it all" to each individual who had been "chosen" to experience the exhibition.

The Paris exhibition of 1889 was one of the most architecturally successful world's fairs. Master builder René Binet created an overall plan incorporating many well-known building symbols: a triumphal arch, a classical portal, and a pillared dome, magically illuminated by thousands of electric lights. Two obelisks stood in front of the fairground's round hall, giving the structure the appearance of a majestic Roman church. The exhibition was built on a site on the Left Bank of the Seine River, with wide stairs leading down to the water.

Around this period, electric lighting, newly invented, was perceived as

Henry Flitcroft, Temple of Flora, 1745.

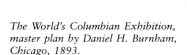

*The World's Columbian Exhibition, master plan by Daniel H. Burnham, Chicago, 1893.*

*Gustave Eiffel,* Eiffel Tower, *created for the World Exhibition in Paris, 1889.*

*The Italian Pavilion at the New York World's Fair, 1939.*

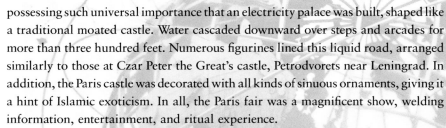

possessing such universal importance that an electricity palace was built, shaped like a traditional moated castle. Water cascaded downward over steps and arcades for more than three hundred feet. Numerous figurines lined this liquid road, arranged similarly to those at Czar Peter the Great's castle, Petrodvorets near Leningrad. In addition, the Paris castle was decorated with all kinds of sinuous ornaments, giving it a hint of Islamic exoticism. In all, the Paris fair was a magnificent show, welding information, entertainment, and ritual experience.

Everything Paris had to offer, however, faded in comparison to the New York World's Fair of 1939–1940. The theme was founded on an illustrious ideal: a better life for mankind through communication and commerce, production and distribution, community interests, food, government, transportation, medicine, science, education, and entertainment. The fair was built around a lake, next to World's Fair Boulevard, now the Long Island Expressway. In addition to Norman Bel Geddes and Henry Dreyfuss, the prominent industrial designers Raymond Loewy and Walter Dorwin Teague participated, as did architects Alvar Aalto, Morris Lapidus, Oscar Niemeyer, and Sven Markelius, joined by the firms of Skidmore & Owings and Shreve, Lamb & Harmon. The entire design team worked on the realization of the underlying concept of every world's fair: "Building the World of Tomorrow." Of course, the future had to look better than the present; it had to look a little like paradise, in keeping with the traditional American belief in progress.

The futuristic theme was visible in the visitors' center, located in a gigantic sphere-shaped building. Painted a bright white, the structure represented the ideal globe and became the hallmark of the exhibition. The globe was dedicated to democracy, a form of government whose ideals the United States wanted to spread around the world. A newly constructed obelisk, tapering to a very sharp point—a project by Francis Kelly and Leonard Dean—stood next to the visitors' center, uniting the symbol of the earth, the sphere, with the energy of the sun.

The spherical form of a building harkened back to the famous *House of the Groundskeeper,* painted in 1785 by Claude Nicolas Ledoux, in which the house resembled a spaceship landed on earth. Moreover, it continued the tradition of an association between dome and obelisk, known from churches in Rome and, in a corrupted form, from English formal gardens, among them the garden at Chiswick.

In New York the association between sphere and obelisk was carried to the absolute limit. This particular world's fair had not only global, but cosmic pretensions. Two large Corona Gates and two bridges "guided" visitors to the site. The

bridge on the left led to the Street of Wheels, the one on the right to the Street of Wings. The streets ran into the Court of Communication and the Court of Power, to the left and the right of the spherical house. Statues scattered around these court-yards, the work of sculptor John Gregory, represented the *Four Victories: Wheels, Wheat, Wings,* and *Wisdom.* The cosmic concept of the exhibition was extended further by the design and designation of the streets that radiated from the spherical house: Constitution Mall formed a central axis, together with the Avenue of Patriots and the Avenue of Pioneers, named after the men and women responsible for the founding of the United States.

Constitution Mall, intersected by Rainbow Avenue—a joining of cosmic significance—opened out on the monuments of the four freedoms, the Lagoon of Nations, and the Court of Peace. The street ended with a flourish: a monumental building, dedicated to the government of the United States, crowned the exhibition site.

If one compares the New York World's Fair with Stourhead in England, it becomes clear that in New York the emphasis had shifted from the individual to "the people." The purpose of Stourhead's itinerary was to guide the individual to self-knowledge and a Christian life. At the New York World's Fair, the intention was to instruct the mass public about the universal meaning of democracy, with its com-mercial and industrial aspirations, in order to nurture patriotic pride in America. Thus, the symbolism of the 1940 New York World's Fair resembled that of Bruno Taut's 1920 "Holy House." In both plans, the concept of community was more important than the concept of the individual. The main difference between them lay in the political dimensions of the projects; New York refined and expanded Taut's utopian vision.

The traditional architectural shapes of sphere, obelisk, bridge, arch, and tower are by themselves neutral. Only the context in which they are used turns them into *architecture parlante.* Any given architectural form, transferred to a new context, may reveal a different meaning. A world's fair has as many metaphysical symbols as a church or an eighteenth-century garden. The fair's symbols are temporary—the duration of the exhibition—and they may function in a more commercial and propagandistic way. Nonetheless, the architectural language of a structure, whether transient or permanent, has the potential to excite imagination, heighten fantasy, and transform vision.

Norman Bel Geddes, General Motors Futurama, New York World's Fair, 1939. Visitors in their moving chairs looking down on America as envisioned in the year 1960.

Peter Muller-Munk, Inc., The Unisphere, symbol of New York World's Fair, 1964.

# EXHIBITIONITIS

## A CONTEMPORARY MUSEUM AILMENT

*Johanne Lamoureux*

Gardens and museums. They are discussed everywhere. More museums are being built, and they are bigger than ever before, with gardens for sculpture and parties. Gardens themselves are being restored, converted into museums, or complemented with museums. Gardens and museums are subjects of special issues of art periodicals and interior design magazines, of scholarly essays, monographs, and coffee-table books. They are even the subjects of art exhibitions. Why are gardens and museums such a fashionable topic; or, to phrase the question more accurately, why do we choose to remember *now* how interconnected they have been throughout history?

On the most superficial level, the renewed interest in gardens coincides with the world's preoccupation with ecology. Indeed, gardens provide us with an ideal ground for formalizing our ambivalent relationship with nature: they embody outdated dreams of gentrification or fantasies of alternative and experimental micro societies. They help some of us mourn our lost belief that there is such a thing as nature, while they allow others to cling to an idealistic concept of nature and grieve over the damages it has endured. Gardens cater to our desire to flee our polluted world and provide a magnet for health faddists and yuppies—a contemporary response to Voltaire's motto *cultivons notre jardin.*

Our current infatuation with gardens, a symptom of the accelerated privatization that has resumed with a new frenzy in the present decade, focuses only occasionally on public parks. Currently, the public is more fascinated with the meditative aspect of oriental gardens, the manicured naturalness of picturesque gardens, and the grand setting of princely gardens. If new gardens do not proliferate these days, it is because we are more interested in the forms of imagination that gardens have stimulated in the past. Ideas of gardens and images of gardens entice us more than gardens themselves.

Museums are also having a veritable resurrection: at no time since the birth of the institution have they been such a subject of concern. I remember a time when I was a student, some ten years ago, indulging in the thought that museums were dead, done with, because art was no longer being produced for them. I, my fellow students, and some of the faculty candidly thought that museums would starve to death. Instead, when artists rejected them, museums were forced to modify their strategies. They have emerged with a stronger ego. Not content to remain neutral spaces, they have rejected the modernist paradigm of a box with white walls and no architectural distractions. They have begun to assert themselves.

Almost any contemporary space is a potential museum. Slaughterhouses,

*The Metropolitan Museum of Art, Chinese garden, recreated detail of a Soochow garden. Built by twenty-five Chinese craftsmen, the garden was transported from China to New York and opened in 1981.*

*Allan McCollum, Surrogate Paintings, 1980–82. The work of McCollum represents the anger and frustration the artist feels about the content and display of works of art in contemporary museums.*

*Art and Language, Index: Incident in a Museum XIII, 1986. The painting refers to the museum as a place in which Modernism is interpreted and often falsified.*

castles, plants, abbeys, railway stations, and even shopping malls are being converted into museum spaces. Museums are being planned on sites with difficult topography, their exhibition spaces redesigned in the latest architectural fashion. Invited to admire the constantly expanded circuit of museums, the museum goer becomes part of a museological conspiracy that merges the eighteenth-century grand tour with the medieval pilgrimage. He no longer knows if, when spring and summer come, he will be running off to pay homage to the relics or be struck dumb by the cathedrals in which they are housed. I suspect that the cathedrals are winning at this new game. Museums today are not primarily repositories of collections; they are feats of architecture or cunning displays of curatorial virtuosity.

### ART FURNITURE

In May 1988, the new National Gallery of Canada finally opened to the public in a palatial postmodern space in Ottawa. For years, the art community had complained that the national collection did not have a proper home. The irony is that the expense of maintaining the "palace" will probably prevent the National Gallery from ever again having the funds to improve its collection. Canada seems to have acquired a giant home without furniture.

The public has learned to think of museums as more than homes for artworks. If proof were needed for the ideological and political implications embedded in the excitement surrounding museological architecture, the National Gallery of Canada, located just behind the Parliament and echoing its silhouette in a transparent glass and steel structure, offers us a rare and almost too-obvious-to-be-true example. It no longer suffices to say that museum architecture has a representational function; it also serves as a colossal and free-floating sign of culture meant to attract visitors, whether or not they care about the art housed within.

Confronted with this situation, one cynically thinks that the dream of the seventies for art institutions has symbolically been realized, but reversed in the process, through an unpredictable mutation. The desire for an informal building without a permanent collection or with a collection of nonobjective art has given way to monumental structures that proudly present traveling exhibitions.

Undeniably, in the mediatory image they have fabricated for themselves, museums have chosen to modulate their commitment to collecting in the relentless pursuit of entrepreneurial exhibitions. The shift from collecting to exhibiting is best illustrated by the blockbuster exhibition.

*The National Gallery of Canada, Ottawa, designed by Moshe Safdie, 1988. The National Gallery, the Museum of Civilization, the Ottawa River, and the Parliament Buildings on the same site are the main tourist attractions of Ottawa.*

Museum exhibitions—or the rhetoric of presentation inherent in exhibitions—are the main focus of our reconsideration of the relationship between gardens and museums. In their theoretical foundations and in their specific requirements from the visitor, gardens invite comparison with museums. Both are champions of the art of layout.

The seventeenth-century gardens of Versailles, already following a well-established custom, included a *cabinet des antiques*, an open-air gallery displaying replicas of the most famous sculptures from antiquity. A text, written by Louis XIV as a guide to ambassadors' visits to the gardens, suggests that they were more than an extravagant stage for the celebrations of absolute monarchy. In their well-orchestrated and well-ordered presentation of artworks, rare flowers and animals, and feats of engineering, they displayed the king's wish to include in his gardens a literal or allegorical representation of everything "under the sun."[1]

During the eighteenth-century the encyclopedic ambition and microcosmic conception of the garden came under attack. The very fact that they were vilified indicates that such opinions still enjoyed the favor of landowners newly converted to gardening practices. In his *Gardens,* written in 1782,[2] Jacques Delille describes the museological pretensions of some gardens. The marquis de Girardin, echoing Jean-Jacques Rousseau's *Nouvelle Héloïse,* expressed similar complaints in his 1777 treatise, written some years after he had started working on his own garden at Ermenonville, outside of Paris:

*It was believed that a great variety could be produced through crowding on a small lot productions from all climates, monuments from every century and through cooping up, so to speak, the whole universe.*[3]

Hubert Robert, Le Parc d'Ermenonville, *1786–90. Robert's paintings of ruins and gardens show how the terrain of the landscape was conceived of as a canvas.*

Girardin was protesting against the exaggerated number of pavilions in some English gardens, laid out to accommodate a variety of well-established formats. Some were architectural, like the Chinese pagoda, the Palladian bridge, the ancient temple, the medieval ruin, or the rustic cottage; others were topographical, like the desert, the island, the pond, and the waterfall. The *topoi* of the English garden were often compressed into a predictable pattern or arranged on a property so small that all *fabriques* interfered with one another and jeopardized the current ideal of verisimilitude. However, Girardin had his own view of how gardens and exhibitions were related. He thought of the terrain as a canvas and spoke of the garden as a "gallery of small pictures" requiring the visitor to walk from one to the

**118**

*Daniel Buren, C'est ainsi et autrement (It's Like This and That), Kunsthalle, Bern, 1983. With his series of invisible paintings, Buren criticizes the institutionalization of art and the censoring of artists by art organizers.*

other "as if behind the frames."[4] Obviously, the picturesque garden led to a rejection of the ostentatiously enclosed garden. The most well-known example of this change is found in the substitution of ha-has—sunken fences—for imposing wrought-iron grills demarking the limits of one's garden. As enclosing devices, ha-has facilitated the garden's melding with the surrounding landscape.

The difference between Louis XIV's concept of the garden and Girardin's lies in the fact that the allegorical program of the garden no longer determined the visitor's orientation or the "success" of his visit. The *promeneur*, or stroller, making the connection between the different "pictures" of the garden, becomes the person who endows the experience with meaning. Gardens moved from semantics to pragmatics.

With this shift in mind, let us reflect on how exhibitions function. Such a consideration urgently requires our attention if only because most of the coverage that the museum gets today is determined by the so-called blockbuster exhibitions. If blockbusters are a treat for art journalism, they are nevertheless far from raising in the press, the critics, or the public, any sensitivity to the curatorial role of conceiving and installing exhibitions. This is not surprising. The success of blockbusters relies more on clever marketing than on exposing the semantics or the rhetoric of the exhibition. The museum has only to exhibit the work of a famous artist, or one rarely shown, newly discovered, or associated with a popular stylistic label like Surrealism or Impressionism, and immediately art historians perform their traditional routines. Through their phenomenal success, blockbusters provide a smoke screen, allowing museums to remain fundamentally the same without having to face any epistemological challenge. The demagogical stance of the blockbuster may lead us to believe that the museum has at last "opened up," but this so-called opening perpetuates an obsolete and traditional discourse on art that would otherwise have collapsed.

*The Museum Shop, Metropolitan Museum of Art, New York, 1989. The constellation of books, postcards, objects d'art, prints, posters, and children's toys often receives the same attention from the museum goer as the works of art.*

## FROM SESAME STREET TO PEE-WEE'S PLAYHOUSE

To exemplify the change in conception that has swept the wonderful Epcot world of mega-exhibitions, one has only to compare the first exhibitions held in the late 1970s to early 1980s at the Centre Georges Pompidou ("Paris-New York," "Paris-Berlin," "Paris-Moscou") with a recent one ("Vienne: La Naissance d'un Siècle"). In their titles they subtly differ: the former stressed *relations* between centers; the latter announced a closed micro-milieu, chronologically anchored in the first third of the twentieth century.

The Paris-X series were bookish exhibitions. The viewer's labyrinthine marathon was slowed down by what the walls relentlessly offered him to read. Documentaries, videos, and other sources of information daringly disrupted the sanctity of the exhibition area. These exhibitions had didactic claims.

With the Vienna exhibition, the mood changed. The exhibition space was no longer an area for reading but a hybrid environment for experimenting. Even the catalog had undergone an unprecedented inflation, curiously symbolized by a reproduction on its cover of Gustav Klimt's pregnant woman, *Hope II*.[5]

Walls were by no means without words in "Vienne." A "Viennese" quotation introduced each room of the exhibition. In one room a visitor could read: "Woman is nothing. This is why she can become everything." A little further along the route, he could ponder: "The streets of Vienna are paved with culture: everywhere else asphalt is already being used." One was left with the choice to draw or not to draw meaning from the clash of these aphorisms.

The intent of the quotations varied, depending upon the rooms with which they were linked; sometimes it was ironic, other times emblematic, antithetic, or, more exceptionally, informative. The connection between the quotations and the themes of each room echoed the relationship between the artifacts on display and the exhibition décor. The décor for "Vienne" was a hybrid setting operating through a wide variety of modalities.

In his essay on the poetics of the museum,[6] the British cultural historian Stephen Bann contrasted the early nineteenth-century exhibition procedures of Alexandre Lenoir at the Musée des Petits-Augustins in Paris, with the system implemented by Alexandre Du Sommerard at the Musée de Cluny. Lenoir arranged his museum around an equation of a room per century. In each room he exhibited a chaotic series of typical artifacts or fragments, bearing no relation to one another except for their similar dates. A few years later, Du Sommerard shifted the arrangement of artifacts from Lenoir's metonymical display, toward a synecdochic one. He

*Sesame Street at the Met: Don't Eat the Pictures, produced by The Children's Television Workshop, 1983. Audio-visual production, including audio tours, video tapes and slides, is a key strategy museums use to engage visitors.*

The catalog Vienne: Naissance d'un Siècle, published in 1986 to accompany the exhibition at the Centre Georges Pompidou, sold 45,000 copies in the three months the exhibition was open.

mounted reconstructions that he hoped would be exemplary:

*In the Room of François I, objects have been allotted their respective places. Not only do all of them come from one period, but they are distributed according to a rational and intelligible economy: the central table, though well-covered, is covered with objects that belong on tables, like books and gaming dice. . . . We have no need for a learned guide in this new context: the historical portrait, presumably one of François I himself, seems to place the whole room under the honorary, mute guardianship of the regal figure who is evoked, synecdochically, by the combined reference of all the objects assembled there.*[7]

In his conclusion, Bann suggests that the poetics of the modern museum "lie in the aternation of [these] two strategies":

*Passages and rooms devoted to the metonymic sequence of schools and centuries are interrupted by "reconstructed" rooms, offering the synecdochical treat of a salon transported from the Ile Saint-Louis, or a dining-room from a departed Jacobean manor-house. Perhaps the automatic way in which the ordinary museum-goer shifts between these two modes implies a modern replacement for the synecdochic and the metonymic museums: the ironic museum, in which we oscillate between the different varieties of imaginative projection that are required.*[8]

The sequential layout of the postmodern exhibition relies on a broader scope of strategies and is not as tightly articulated in a dialectical fashion as the model proposed by Bann. The specific typology of the "Vienne" décor supports this assumption. On the one hand, a symbolic arch stood in the red-walled room devoted to Communist Vienna. On the other, a purely ornamental pergola of glass paste and *trompe l'oeil* marbles served perfunctorily as a divider between two parts of another room. One could also discover a fetishist presentation of Sigmund Freud: a closet-size, dark room, which it was forbidden to enter, displayed a golden miniature couch and chair on a pedestal in front of a copy of the Gradiva bas-relief. In the realm of reconstructions alone there were diverse methods of presentation. A typical salon of the period was evoked by a few accessories, such as a grand piano, green plants, and a draped ceiling. Otto Wagner's metro station was partially reconstructed. A papered wall from Peter Altenberg's room at the Graben Hotel was displayed with various framed photographs, including, if one looked closely, a photograph of the original room, which served as a model for the reconstruction.

Some reconstructions merely provided a context in which to view objects.

*The exhibition "Vienne, Naissance d'un Siècle" was the major cultural event in Paris in 1986. Some 600,000 visitors saw the exhibition.*

*The exhibition designer of Vienne: Naissance d'un Siècle, Gerard Regnier, characterized the exhibition as one in which the visitor "entered through Sissi clichés and left with a nightmarish impression."*

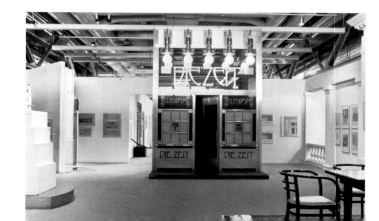

For example, the room dealing with the crafts of the Wiener Werkstatte, a collaborative effort by the Hans Hollein Workshop, was a simulated environment designed to entice the visitor. Gray walls, wall-to-wall carpeting, crystal chandeliers, and windows sparkling with the silverware, glassware, and jewelry designed by the artists of the movement surrounded one in an atmosphere reminiscent of Tiffany's.

In the leaflet sold as a guide to the exhibition, one could read about the contradictions in the Viennese crafts movement: the group wished to create affordable products but ultimately designed goods accessible only to a wealthy clientele. No written explanation of this dichotomy could be found in the Wiener Werkstatte room, but the setting itself created a situation in which the contradiction might dawn on viewers, exposed to items they could only covet, not own. On the other hand, the setting could also reinforce their alienation, expressed in a symphony of frustrated and admiring sighs. If the visitor was not fortunate enough to be able to afford the various replicas of the period for sale in the museum store, he could still compensate with a Viennese pastry from the simulated Viennese café, conveniently located in front of the store.

The sequence of the rooms in "Vienne" was arranged to exacerbate contrasts of ambiances. The impression orchestrated by such unpredictable changes of tone and rhetoric resembled a ride on an emotional roller coaster. One visited "Vienne," the exhibition, like one would have strolled through Vienna, the city. In "Vienne," the décor of the exhibition replaced the Paris-X legends that supported the

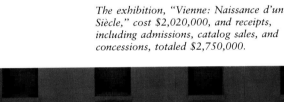

*The exhibition, "Vienne: Naissance d'un Siècle," cost $2,020,000, and receipts, including admissions, catalog sales, and concessions, totaled $2,750,000.*

*The Centre Georges Pompidou reported that the exhibition "Vienne: Naissance d'un Siècle" was "pure visualization" provoking "physical sensations." The "Café Viennois," installed within the museum, served 5,000 people a day.*

didactic treatment of ideas and themes. It provided a matrix for a possible, but also totally dispensable, reading of the exhibition, however fragmented and intermittent that reading might be. The décor served as a mediator between the poles of emission—the making, hanging, or installation of the works—and reception—the itinerary, or movement, of the visitor.

Mediation of the décor can be hindered by several obstacles. The visitor's customary viewing habits work against his being receptive to judging or interpreting exhibited work. For example, department stores and television regularly drown us in a variety of displays and formats that very few people feel compelled to make sense of. Variety can numb, or it can be just entertaining; it does not structurally stimulate or guarantee interaction between producer and audience.

Then, too, there are already many exhibitions in which the décor has trivialized other curatorial functions, among them critical responsibility and the ability to conceptualize the reasons for presenting the material in a particular way. The "look" of exhibitions has become preeminent partly because the other curatorial functions are so highly disputed. Can the installation of works of art assert itself as a reading of the works?

In a recent issue of *Cahiers d'Art Moderne*, in an article titled "L'Oeuvre et Son Accrochage," edited in conjunction with a Pompidou exhibition of the same title, Claire Stoullig complained about the press's lack of attention to installations of works of art.[9] She attributed its indifference to a failure to appreciate how an exhibition's narrative—its form and content—is determined by the way the curator installs the artworks. In the same issue, Daniel Buren denounced the practice of installation in which the curator and the artist become co-authors of the exhibition, rather than the artist and the viewer.[10] (Buren advocates that artists should not delegate the installation of their work to curators. Indeed, many artworks, even those claiming not to be site-specific, possess in their very structure a consideration for the problems of installation; Allan McCollum's framed black canvases or vases, for example, emphasize our gratuitous displaying of commodities.)

The dilemma raised by the relationship of the curator, the artist, and the viewer is best formulated by the question, "Should this situation be avoided?" rather than "Can this situation be avoided?" Even installations acknowledged to be sensitively compatible with the exhibited artworks still propose a "reading" of these works, still impose on the viewers the curator's conception of the work. Any installation channels the works through a detour. The detour may take the form of a parasitic juxtaposition of artworks, of an obscure or obvious sequence of works in succeeding rooms, of a certain number of works in a given room, of an arbitrary placing of chairs in front of certain works, of a choice of color and lighting for walls and ceilings. The detour can also involve the omission of works—a more insidious obstacle.

The problem does not lie in the detour itself; it surfaces when curators fail to see installations for what they unmistakably are—interpretations. One regrets, along with Buren, that curators rarely acknowledge in print why they have chosen particular works to exhibit and what constitutes the underlying conception in their presentation.[11]

Such a discourse would probably hamper the current habit, among some curators, of orchestrating *effets de sens* by placing works next to each other for decorative, formal reasons that have nothing to do with content. In such cases, the installation transmutes the artworks into the very décor of the exhibition, a décor whose purpose is to disguise the emptiness of the curatorial statement. Making sense of the exhibition is thus left up to the viewer.

The installation-as-décor-as-narrative evolves from one end of the extreme polarization between two modes of contemporary curatorship: the exhibition-as-décor and the exhibition-as-concept. The former is in favor because of the current belief that it is legitimate to exhibit just about anything. At the same time, however, there is no consensus on how material should be presented. For curators to delegate the responsibility of the exhibition's statement to the décor is a real temptation. In the worst scenario of exhibition-as-décor, the works are presented in a way that emotionally manipulates the viewers along a picturesque route of unrelated "moments."

The exhibition-as-concept encompasses all exhibitions that illustrate or

*Dennis Oppenheim,* Identity Stretch, *1970–75, executed at Art Park in Lewiston, New York. The idea of scenographic installation, and the new mobility of artists and spectators led in the 1970s to the growth of site-specific art.*

*Bertrand Lavier,* Accrochage no. 2, *1986, installed at Le Consortium, Dijon, 1986. The artist questions uniqueness versus the expendable and the irreplaceable versus the expandable in this work.*

"play" along with a preconceived curatorial script. These are the exhibitions for which artists are asked to create specific works, a practice that Jean-Marc Poinsot, the French art historian and critic, has called "event specificity."[12] In the worst scenario of these exhibitions, the artworks are a mere pretext for the exercise of the curator's ego. The viewers are robbed of the opportunity to recognize how artworks resist complying with the curatorial script.

To prevent a further split between exhibition-as-décor and exhibition-as-concept we seriously need, no matter how chaotic the investigation might prove to be, more exhibitions that take up the challenge of examining in a forthright manner how the décor functions as a concept.

### POSTINDEXICAL INSTALLATIONS

This article attempts to show how the model of the picturesque garden can be applied to recent mega-exhibitions. I first became aware of "picturesque" curators while reviewing major contemporary exhibitions in Europe from 1984 to 1986 for *Parachute* magazine.[13] To understand further how the picturesque serves contemporary exhibitions, one must also investigate installation art itself.

Installation art in the eighties[14] is no longer determined, as it was in the seventies, by the specific physical qualities of a particular site. A certain indifference toward the physicality of the location, and even the contingencies of the work, have replaced the indexical marking of a space. Installations today are often movable pieces, not the least ephemeral, transported from exhibition to exhibition, sometimes with slight, timely adaptations to fit a more peculiar context.

The new mobility of installation art has created an emphasis on the different components of a work rather than on the relationship between site and work. As the syntactical liaison gains strength, the site often functions as a more or less neutral background or as one element among others. It is sometimes echoed in certain motifs of the installation, but almost as decoration or to capitalize on the ambiance of a historical building or deserted factory. The physical relationship of work to site gives way to the creation of a psychological climate or kind of architectural punning. The installation awaits the beholder, wandering through the exhibition, to make connections between its evocative fragments.

These modifications in installation art reactivate the notion of disposition: distributing elements in a given space, without any clash or any disjunction with the site. Disposition reverses the traditional view of installation art. In her "Notes on the

Index"[15] published in 1977 in *October* magazine, Rosalind Krauss associates installation art with a photographic model, which she defines as one emphasizing relationships between work and site. She contrasts the photographic model with the pictorial model, which has as its concern the internal articulation of parts. If one examines installation art of the eighties, it is possible to conclude that the pictorial model has gained preeminence over the photographic model. However, such an interpretation is too simplistic. It implies that the criticism of the pictorial hegemony, spearheaded by many different artists over the last twenty years, has had no effect. For this reason, it is more productive to characterize second-generation installation art as work involving a reconsideration of the picturesque. Calling attention to the picturesque model rather than the pictorial one allows for the possibility that the so-called "return of painting" to the contemporary art scene of the eighties is not a matter of a sudden reassertion of frames, thick impasto, and private iconographies. The return also permeated art practices that no longer dealt with paint, that had liquidated the modernist autonomy of the medium. This infiltration often acknowledged rather than denied the dissolution of medium boundaries following Minimalism.

With Minimal art, the hegemony of the picture approached dissolution. Through the confrontation of the known and the perceived, through the enhancement and duration of the experience, Minimal art induced a new pragmatism. In so doing, it modified the conventions of "pleasure" for the spectator. Minimal art taught us a different form of art experience, one that we soon came to demand. It also established new criteria for judgment. After Minimalism, instead of assuming that a work of art has an objective reality we can instantly grasp, we began to demand that the "journey" itself be one of the conditions of our aesthetic pleasure or interest.

The advent of site specificity, in turn, refashioned the notion of the journey by no longer confining it to the abstract gallery space. In fact, a current practice of the "art of exhibition," exemplified by Jan Hoet's "Chambres d'Amis," stresses the dissolution of the exhibition, its near vanishing into the city. As participants in the exhibition, each artist was invited to produce a work that fit into one of many private spaces throughout Ghent, made available for the duration of the event. The visitor-tourist to the exhibition, with ticket-map in hand, proceeded from house to house, following one of several recommended itineraries.

*Paul Thek, installation at "Chambres d'Amis," Ghent, 1986. The museum invited artists to present works in houses throughout the city. The formula of "Chambres d'Amis" was taken up by art organizers throughout the world.*

*Helmut Middendorf, installation at "Chambres d'Amis," Ghent, 1986. In the 1980s, the museum definition of the word picturesque was replaced by the more colloquial expression "It hangs well in this place."*

*Jef Cornelis,* The Longest Day, *broadcast on the occasion of the opening of "Chambres D'Amis" in Ghent by Belgian Radio and Television on June 21, 1986. The opening was conceived and staged as a media event.*

## RELOCATION OF THE PICTURESQUE

The picturesque garden was the first art form to validate the stroll.[16] It combined an interest in site specificity—then called the "genius of the place"—with a reliance on the visitor, walking from "picture" to "picture" to guarantee the syntactical binding between, for example, a rustic scene and an island of love, a view over the lake reminiscent of Claude Lorrain and a wild, rocky landscape evoking Salvador Rosa.[17] By evoking memories of actual artwork, the picturesque was subservient to the hegemony of painting. At the same time, it challenged and ruptured that hegemony. The picturesque garden constantly reiterated that a picture does not exist in a vacuum, that it is part of a network of pictures, and that, most important, the actual space between pictures has to be taken into account by a stroller.

During the eighteenth century, discourse on the nature of the picturesque changed, quite predictably, from an initial focus on the repertory of picturesque objects to the definition of the picturesque as a mode of vision. William Gilpin[18] in 1772 tried to identify all possible picturesque objects in order to produce guidelines for artists to follow in their choice of subject matter. In his canon, ruins, gnarled trees, waterfalls, and even rough and uneven silhouettes were worthy subjects for paintings. Early in the nineteenth century, the aesthetician Richard Payne Knight[19] exiled the picturesque from the contemplated object and, following Immanuel Kant, relocated it in the mind of the beholder—a culturally educated beholder. In a given landscape the picturesque was no longer a scene to be painted but one for a beholder to reflect on, through memories of paintings and the associations they engender. In this way, the picturesque ushered in a period of mourning for painting. Today, many curators fantasize the ideal visitor as a Knightian daydreamer who will endow with private meaning the unmotivated eclecticism of their sophisticated exhibitions.

[1] J. M. Apostolides, "Fêtes dans les Jardins de Versailles sous Louis X1V," in *Traverses,* 5/6, "Jardins contre Nature." See also Louis XIV, "Manière de Montrer les Jardins de Versailles," Cabinet des Estampes, Bibiothèque Nationale, Paris, Ref: Ve 1318 res.

[2] Jacques Delille, *Les Jardins* (1782; Paris, 1827), 11: 35: "Par-tout entremêlés d'arbres pyramidaux, Marbres, bronzes, urnes, temples, tombeaux Parlent de Rome antique: et la vue abusée Croit, au lieu d'un jardin, parcourir un musée."

[3] R. Girardin, *De la Composition des Paysages* (1777; Paris, 1979), p. 207 (my translation). It is worth noting that this quotation has recently been used as a title for an anthology of texts on exhibitions: J. Davallon, ed., *Claquemurer, pour Ainsi Dire, Tout l'Univers* (Paris: Centre Georges Pompidou [C.C.I.], 1986).

[4] R. Girardin, op. cit., p. 45.

[5]In fact, on the day "Vienne" opened in Paris, the evening news on French television mentioned the impressive publication, and proudly announced its weight as if it were a newborn baby.

[6]Stephen Bann, *The Clothing of Clio* (Cambridge University Press, 1984), Chapter 4: "The Poetic of the Museum: Lenoir and Du Sommerard."

[7]Ibid., p. 87.

[8]Ibid., p. 91.

[9]Claire Stoullig, "La Presse et l'Accrochage," in "L'Oeuvre et Son Accrochage," *Cahiers d'Art Moderne* 17/18, 1986.

[10]Daniel Buren, "La Peinture et Son Exposition ou la Peinture Est-elle Presentable?" op. cit.

[11]Ibid., p. 172.

[12]Jean-Marc Poinsot, unpublished lecture given at a conference on "Les Pratiques in Situ," July 1–2, 1987, Centre Georges Pompidou.

[13]I believe my first encounter with a typically picturesque exhibition was Kasper Konig's "Von hier aus," September 29-December 2, 1984, Dusseldorf. See also *Parachute* 38 (Spring 1985): pp. 32–33.

[14]For a more complete discussion of picturesque installation art in the 1980s, see my "Lieux et Non-lieux du Pittoresque," *Parachute* 39 (Summer 1985): pp. 10–19.

[15]Rosalind Krauss, "Notes on the Index: Seventies Art in America," *October* 3 (Fall 1977).

[16]In the context of postmodernist art criticism, some writers have indeed investigated the issue of the picturesque. See Yves-Alain Bois, "A Picturesque Stroll Around Clara-Clara," *October* 29, and Rosalind Krauss, "The Originality of the Avant-garde: A Post-modernist Repetition," *October* 18. Both writers deliberately avoid considering, in possibly positive terms, the relations between the picturesque and the medium of painting. The picturesque seems to them an interesting or operative concept as long as it can be maintained in isolation from any pictorial concerns. Bois even blames Girardin for being still so attached to a pictorial conception of the picturesque.

[17]"This dark and turning path," writes Girardin, "leads to a site arranged in the Italian taste: it presents a picture, perfectly well-composed, in the manner of Robert" (Hubert Robert, French painter, mostly of ruins, 1733–1808). R. Girardin, op. cit., p. 137.

[18]William Gilpin, *Observations relative chiefly to Picturesque Beauty, made in the year 1772 on several parts of England, particularly the mountains and lakes of Cumberland and Westmoreland* (London: R. Blamire, 1786), 2 vols.

[19]Richard Payne Knight, *Analytical Inquiry into the Principles of Taste* (London, 1805).

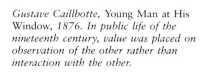

*Gustave Caillbotte,* Young Man at His Window, *1876. In public life of the nineteenth century, value was placed on observation of the other rather than interaction with the other.*

*Teo Zasche, Ringstrasse Corso in Vienna, 1908. The composer Gustav Mahler (with flat hat and white beard) strolls the busy streets, unapproachable by a public who holds him and other artists in awe.*

# The Museum as an Anarchic Experience

## A Conversation Between Richard Sennett and Chris Dercon

*In the fall of 1987 Chris Dercon and television director Stefaan Decostere spent an afternoon in Amsterdam's Arti et Amicitriae, an artists' society, talking to Richard Sennett, author and social historian, about the evolution of the museum and the museumification of the world. The ideas they discussed were incorporated into a script for a television documentary called* The New Museum. *Following is a transcript of their conversation.*

CHRIS DERCON: Let's begin by talking about the changing relationship between the city, the public, and the museum.

RICHARD SENNETT: In the middle of the eighteenth century the public was still a rather small group of people. They were not necessarily people who knew each other, but they were people who shared a common interest in the city in which they lived. In the nineteenth century, what it meant to be *in* public, and the definition of the public, changed. Cities grew much larger, and the public itself became more of an enigma; it couldn't identify what it stood for because it was composed of different classes with different tastes and desires. That confusion really affected the relationship of people as a public of arts. When they went to concerts, to the theater, or to the great expositions in London, for example, they became more and more passive. That is to say, the public became more and more heterogenous, more and more unknown to itself when it became a public in search of culture. The nineteenth century's city that we know from Charles Baudelaire, for instance, is a place in which nobody can relate to anyone else, and the ambiguity of relationships puts a new kind of value on art. People believed that art, that the stage particularly, told the truth about the street, which people were now unable to see for themselves.

This development of the public realm had a terrific impact on creating a public for museums. The museum was only possible when there was a public that wanted to be educated by going to a place for culture. I personally think this is a terrible development. I don't think museums should be places of education. The more a museum becomes a place of education, the more the public in that museum becomes passive. It behaves like a typical nineteenth-century public. I would much rather see museums work confrontationally with the public. I would like to see the public invited to museum exhibitions that don't make sense, that aren't explained, where there is no Walk-man saying: "Now you will move to the next picture and see the following." Even a museum in which it is impossible to find where the exhibit is,

*Jacques Tati,* Trafic, *1971. In his film comedies, Tati comments on the isolation of the individual within the sterile and rigid environment of the modern city.*

*Joseph Stephan, Marketplace of Old Munich, 1760s. Before the realization of the nineteenth century the marketplace had multiple functions in a small town's daily life. Public life was not yet fragmented and dispersed.*

*Square of Art and Sciences, Paris, 1870s. Newly built squares were filled not only with people but carefully placed shrubs and trees, taking on an importance similar to the city's cultural monuments.*

where it begins, and where it ends. Because ultimately the educational museum gives people not a mirror in which to see themselves, but a glass through which they see what might be, if only they could understand themselves.

CD: What would an ideal museum look like?

RS: For one thing, it would not have a permanent collection. Its holdings would travel, always. You wouldn't go to a museum to see something that is housed, which is officially "culture." Museums would be exhibitions. I have a great bias in this area; I really believe André Malraux's "museum without walls." I know it's very easy to deride that idea, but to me it makes enormous sense. The notion that there's a place in which resides a kind of *summa* of culture creates too static a view of a culture's patrimony.

CD: But don't you think that when one talks about "exhibitions" instead of permanent collections, we are moving toward a stage in which works of art are taken hostage, in that they are all subjected to a kind of *mise en scène*? Nowadays a whole set of operations are being used to make exhibitions effective: lighting, acoustics, how you enter and leave the exhibit, the traffic, the rhythm—all are designed to call into question who has the authority over the works of art, the organizers or the public.

*Gustav Klimt, Auditorium of the Altes Burgtheater, Vienna, 1888. In the nineteenth-century city, the organization of public life became more and more specific. People gathered in three locations: the park, the theater, and the café.*

RS: Well, it's interesting to me that in New York and in Paris, a really successful exhibition, as far as the public and the media are concerned, is one that deals authoritatively with everything about a subject. For example, all of Caravaggio in one space, at one time, all laid out as Caravaggio could never have experienced his work. Suddenly he becomes available to the public as a complete package. You could say, that's very educational, you can see the whole *oeuvre*, you can see what the artist never could see about himself. But in another way Caravaggio becomes the ultimate commodity. The parallels between museums and music—and music is an art I know much more about—are striking. Most opera houses are now museums. The *mise en scène*—the sets, the elaborate stage design, the costumes— becomes the experience of opera, to the disastrous effect of the art of singing as something alive. Opera has become a director's opera; that is to say, the only thing to be done with this sacred text is to represent it in a new way. The fact that opera could be something just sung,

*Reinhold Völkel, Café Griensteidl in Vienna, 1870s. In this nineteenth-century café, people congregate, drink, read, converse, and observe, but the artist depicts them as a lonely crowd.*

that it's there on its own, is not sufficient, just as to have a few Caravaggios is not sufficient. One has in some way to put a big frame around the whole work. I would much rather have a museum be a more active kind of confrontational theater.

CD: What do you mean when you talk about confrontational theater?

RS: I mean, historically, eighteenth-century theater audiences were very, very active. They did things like "point" and "settle" actors. When an actor recited very well-known lines, the audience would recite—"point"—them along with him. Settling was a process that was used when an actor or singer didn't perform up to standard; the audience would whistle and hoot and stamp its feet to make him repeat his lines or do a better job. The attitude toward the artist was much more disdainful; people felt artists were there to give pleasure. I think it was Oliver Goldsmith who said, "We aim to please, and we only live by pleasing." That's a much less exalted view than we have of the modern artist. What I'm talking about is a situation in which the audience feels it has more rights. It can only have these rights if the museum itself is not a place where an audience goes to be educated. The audience must have another relationship with the museum, in which there is no attempt to impart knowledge but instead to present something to be judged.

CD: Don't you think the public has changed so much since the eighteenth century that it is not capable of judging works of art anymore?

RS: As we discussed, in the early nineteenth century, you had an active public. After the World Exposition of 1851 in London, that public changed. It was a bigger population going to the Royal Academy, and it expected to be instructed by the arts. It was a more homogenous, bourgeois public.

CD: Why this sudden change?

RS: There are a lot of reasons for it, and they vary from country to country. The system of patronage in England really changed a great deal in the middle of the nineteenth century. Aristocrats stopped buying modern paintings because art ceased to be a status symbol; it entered the capitalist system as a commodity. For the first time a bourgeois public, as well as public institutions including museums, began

*Swain,* Edison's Anti-Gravitation Underclothing, 1879. *Cartoon of imaginary invention by Thomas Alva Edison. In a picture gallery filled with art, art lovers fly up to the ceiling to see the paintings.*

*Anonymous cartoon of art connoisseurs investigating the paintings at the Paris Salon. The increasing number of entries to the salons forced it to move from the Louvre in 1857 to the Palace of Industry, built for the World Exhibition of 1855.*

*Visitors studying sculptures at the Paris Salon of 1897. While the bourgeoisie had increasing access to art at the turn of the century, aesthetic judgment was based not on what one felt personally, but on what highly specialized critics wrote.*

buying paintings. At the same time, great private collections, like the Wallace Collection, were formed, which were then given in toto to the public. The Wallace Collection is an amazing collection, very adventurous for its time; its creator trusted his eye without any external advice and sought to assemble pictures with what he called "a secret unity" from all periods. The moment it was seen in public, it became a standard. It was no longer one man's adventure in looking at painting, but a definition of what was important at a certain moment.

Instead of establishing the certainties of social life, art gradually became taxed with putting into an expressive form impersonal experience that people couldn't find explanations for themselves. You can see this change, for instance, in nineteenth-century psychology, which began as a kind of enlightened psychology of human character. As the century progressed, the theory of personality developed. It was hypothesized that people have immanent personalities that develop over the years. If that's the case and you are in a realm with other people in which everything is problematic, mysterious, how do you know who you are? How do you know what your personality is? Its deathly when the public says about artists: "Well, they know what feeling is about. They know how to feel. They know how to express feelings in their pictures." That's part of the way in which works of art gather authority: they interpret not what is true but what is real emotionally to people. It's very bad for an artist to take on that kind of authority; it's bad for the amount of experimentation he or she has in the work. It's a kind of museumification. The museumification of art means that artists begin looking at themselves as blocks of marble. They believe they must represent themselves in an authoritative way to the public. They come to believe they can't make mistakes, that the work must cohere. Suddenly the public begins thinking, "Well, does it all fit together?" In fact, it never does, and it shouldn't. An artist is accepting himself as an authority, a commodity when he's able to talk about the development of his work. That kind of self-consciousness indicates he has made himself fit for museums. And the more authority we grant to art and to the artist, the more passivity we can expect from the public.

CD: With the Dada movement of the early twentieth century, and the first avant-garde exhibitions, the public at least was offered a chance to be an active participant again. This didn't happen. Why not?

RS: No, it didn't. It's interesting to compare the outrage at *Déjeuner sur l'Herbe* or

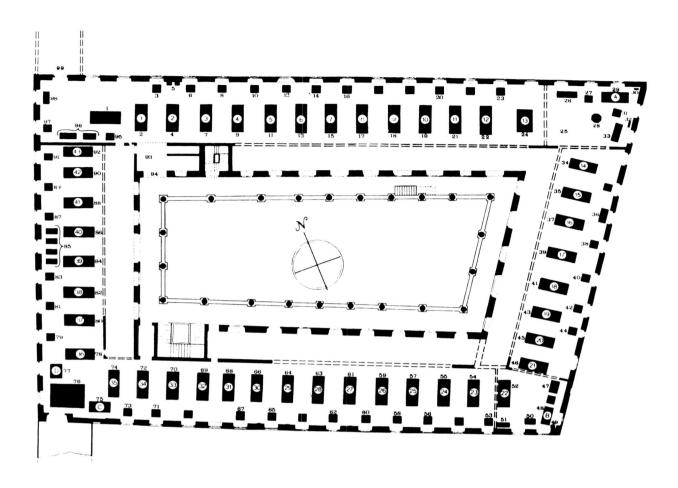

*Olympia* by Manet with the expressions of outrage at Dada. Scorn was poured on Manet, but fear was expressed vis-à-vis Dada. Fear is the measure of a passive public. The reaction to the *Olympia* is the last time you see traces of an active public in the *ancien régime* sense. Look, I love to be loved; every artist does. Still, I would rather arouse derision than fear. It would be more fun for me. It is bad for artists to have the feeling that they are expected to *épater le bourgeoisie* in the sense of showing it what it never knew about itself. No human being should ever take that kind of stance toward other people. It's an arrogance that is stultifying: "I know about you what you don't know about yourself."

CD: Why don't we have more subjective lighting in exhibitions? Why not create a playfulness with light, instead of demanding that it look "natural"?

RS: I'll tell you a rather nice story. Friends of mine were looking at a painting that I have in a corner of my house. Somebody said to me, "You should have this better lit."

*Gärtner, plan of Munich Kunstkammer, 1807, based on an inventory of 1598, showing cabinets with* Kunstkammerstücke. *"Kunstkammerstück" is an object of remarkable character or quality chosen, ordered, or commissioned for display.*

*Jardin des Plantes, Paris, eighteenth century. The Jardin des Plantes was a garden, a zoo, and a museum. It was a scientific laboratory whose evolution paralleled the development of the nineteenth-century city.*

*Michael Curtiz,* The Mystery of the Wax Museum, *1933. Madame Tussaud with her uncle established a Wax Portrait Gallery in 1780 in the Palais Royale, Paris, in which wax heads of prominent persons in the Revolution were displayed.*

And I thought, "Why does something need to be well lit?" If I want to have light, I'll just move a lamp to shine on it. Why make such a fetish of it? I think a relaxed attitude toward being able to get to a work of art easily is a more artful attitude than one insisting on perfect display. You can't imagine taking a lamp into the Louvre and holding it up to see a painting better. We expect lighting, we expect a *mise en scène* in a museum to do the work of interpretation for us.

CD: But then you contradict yourself.

RS: I frequently do.

CD: You said earlier that you wanted to see a more theatrical look to exhibitions, that exhibitions should look more like theater. Theater is still about directing something or acting something. If you want to have a more theatrical style to exhibitions, you are obliged to work with architecture that involves pacing, lighting, and even elaborate acoustics.

RS: I don't agree. I don't think theater is at all about *mise en scène*. I think it's about ritual, a ritual between the audience and the actor. It can be badly lit, the actors can have terrible costumes, they can forget their lines, and none of it matters. Theater happens at the moment in which a feeling passes between the actor and the audience.

CD: How should we ritualize exhibitions?

RS: For one thing, the exhibition should not have a catalog. The paintings would be identified on the wall, perhaps, but there would not be a catalog. The public might enter the exhibition from several directions, instead of going from room A to B to C. The point of the exhibition would be not to display objects, but to present a problem, not to make something coherent but something that is purposely contradictory or provocative. The public would say, "I don't understand this." Nonetheless, they would be engaged.

CD: Are you describing a reinvestment in the idea of the artist's studio?

RS: Yes. That's a good way to put it. The studio is, I would think, a better model of

The Approach to the Art Museum, *a nineteenth-century engraver's fantasy about what a visit to the museum of the future might be like.*

the museum than the concept we have now. However, this notion means smaller exhibitions; it means breaking up collections.

CD: But then we go again into the realm of the private and the public because in the nineteenth century the studio was a public space, wasn't it?

RS: Some studios were, and some weren't. Early in the nineteenth century, the studio was the principal outlet through which a painter sold his work. You didn't need a *droit d'entrée*. People went to the studio, and the painter wanted as many people there as he could accommodate. The studio was his gallery and his working space at the same time. The day before the artist had an exhibition he opened his studio for a private viewing—the *vernissage*—for important people like critics, connoisseurs, and potential buyers. Through word of mouth, in salons and coffee shops, this private sector gave judgments that oriented the public. The studio *vernissage* gradually became a social event, its locus changing to the larger and more spectacular space of the museum. At the same time, artists less and less opened their studios to *vernissage* because they found other ways to sell their work. The act of creating became more private, and, consequently, more secret. It's always a surprise to read about the working habits of both painters and musicians in the eighteenth century. Mozart never worked in private. He talked to friends while he scribbled. Sir Joshua Reynolds had people to dinner while he worked; he accepted that other things could be going on while he made art. Our acceptance of the idea that the artist has to work in secret contributes to our sense that the work itself has authority.

CD: Let's go back to your remarks about exhibition catalogs. Why are you so opposed to them? Do you think that the catalog is too instructional, or a souvenir, or a guidebook?

RS: It depends which ones you're talking about. If you are buying a record of an exhibition, that's one thing. But the kinds of catalogs that are now being written, with titles like *Manet and His World*, for example, are meant to be instructional. The amount of literary material describing one particular painting is incredible. What we call instruction is a kind of repression of the viewer's own impression. The work of art will survive the fact that the viewer may have very bad, even wrong information, that he or she may have completely silly interpretations. It doesn't

*Zoo, Regent's Park, London, 1851. Some 145,000 visitors visited the zoo in 1851, which was a short walk across the park from Madame Tussaud's Wax Museum.*

*The Museum of John Soane, the Dome, London. Sir John Soane lived in the house he designed specifically for his antiquities. The heterogeneous art fragments were meant to be an aesthetic experience rather than a scientific one.*

matter. What matters is that he is engaged in trying to interpret the work.

CD: The Dutch architect Rem Koolhaas has said that his ideal museum would be an empty space, as large as a football field, with a mass of spectators on line at the entrance, much the way people line up at the Lenin Mausoleum. How should museums treat the spectator? Should they send the public invitations to their openings? Should they treat the public more aggressively?

RS: The Lenin Mausoleum is the most bourgeois idea I can imagine for a museum. If you want to create more museums like it, it's easy to do. The public is just waiting to line up to get into them. I would like to see museums go in a more informal direction. If the means of exposing the arts become more informal, less instructional, we all benefit. Creating order for the public leads to Stalinism; Stalinism is the ultimate bourgeois form. I would like museum going to be a more anarchic experience, because it actively involves the spectator.

CD: Do you see an evolution in the public's response to the arts from the beginning of the twentieth century through, let's say, the sixties?

RS: What is interesting about the sixties as a time for the arts is that participation became a substitute—a bad substitute—for interpretation. The artist—and I'm most aware of this in the theater of the sixties—and the public shared one experience; they interacted in such a way that they became a unit. The public was supposedly participating actively—I'm thinking of happenings, for example—but there was no provocation to the public. You had a new version of passivity in which everybody was together and no one was exposed. The Living Theater was, I think, the only theater group that surmounted this "togetherness," and they surmounted it because they believed very much, like Jerzy Grotowski and his Polish "poor theater," that theater is a ritual. They didn't ask the public to perform; they didn't ask the public to become actors; there was no discussion of what the theater means.

A work of art is idiosyncratic, and it should illicit an idiosyncratic reaction. Community is not activity. Creating an artistic community in which the viewer and the artists have an agreeable relationship, a friendly relationship, is very bad for the artist. He becomes passive and so does the public. In the sixties the act of being together replaced the interpretive act of a viewer saying, "Do I like this?" "What is

Studio of Gertrude and Leo Stein, rue du Fleurus, Paris, 1906. Through the exclusion of the avant-garde from official public collections, artists such as Picasso depended almost exclusively upon private patrons such as the Steins.

136

going on here?" Instead, you had a dialogue that tended to be very polite. I remember doing a theater piece in 1966 and actually stopping at the end of each act to talk with the audience about the performance. We asked the audience, "How did you feel when the actors did such and such?" Well, people would offer opinions, but since the actors were present, their remarks didn't have any bite. Then the actors talked about what they were trying to do. The result was very flat.

CD: Today, museums are repositories of classification, of different forms of interpretation. Similar objects can be organized in many different ways because they have been disconnected from their semantic value. For example, by putting a Henri Laurens next to a Georges Braque and another Braque next to another Laurens, the museum is telling the public how to interpret these works; it is suggesting influences or a particular development. This is interpretation on a very primitive level, which one might compare to the idea of *jardins zoologiques.* The public doesn't go to exotic zoos or gardens to see just one species; it goes to see a collection of different species, from different genera, living on different continents.

RS: Well, I think museums would give viewers a stronger interpretation if they didn't group modern art in the same rooms but followed the example of London's National Gallery, which has a program that invites artists to go through its collection and put together, for example, a Vermeer next to a Mondriaan, next to a Chardin. But that would be a very strong interpretation, which I think the public would resist, because it would require too much of them. "Why are these paintings together?" they would ask themselves. To my mind, this would be a more interesting museum.

CD: Why do you say Vermeer, Chardin, Mondriaan?

RS: I don't know. I just see them together. I know they go together in some way. I'm thinking about how Roland Barthes's mind functions. In *Mythologies,* he puts the most unlikely things together, like astrology and detergents. That isn't what you see in most museums. You see taxonomy—pictures grouped for the most obvious reasons—and taxonomy means you don't have to think.

CD: By putting a seventeenth-century Vermeer next to an eighteenth-century Chardin next to a twentieth-century Mondriaan, the museum creates a narrative in

Daniel Buren, C'est ainsi et autrement (It's Like This and That), *Kunsthalle Bern, 1983. Buren states that the topic of an exhibition is no longer the exhibition of works of art, but the exhibition itself as the work of art.*

Jerzy Grotowski, Polish avant-garde theater director, used space dynamics in his Theater Laboratory productions. In the 1960s Grotowski abolished the distance between the actor and the audience by eliminating the conventional proscenium stage.

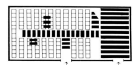

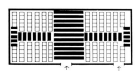

Jerzy Grotowski, drawing for stage production. The director evoked a mental hospital with the audience and actors assuming the roles of the patients.

retrospect. Do you think it's important that it do this?

RS: Yes, because one of the primary ways in which we interpret something is not by remembering it as it was, but by creating a memory. From reading Proust we know that the recovery of the past involves active remembering, and active remembering is always influenced by what is occurring in the present. Proust makes a wonderful statement about viewing Vermeer's *View of Delft*. He writes that had he been younger he couldn't have viewed it because at that time his suffering was too intense. He would have asked too much from the painting. Our memories always operate actively. In the English language we make a distinction between recall and memory. Recall is, "What was it like exactly in 1722?" But memory is, "Why do I want to go back there?" In 1986, Frank Stella wrote a great art book concerning memory called *Working Space*, about Caravaggio "remembered" from the time of Jackson Pollock, not Caravaggio as he actually was, but the Caravaggio it is necessary to remember if one is trying to understand Pollock. A taxonomic museum doesn't let us remember; it only lets us recall by becoming a repository of the past, like the Lenin Mausoleum.

CD: Another model of the museum as a mausoleum confronting us today is television. Theater festivals, music festivals, cinema festivals, blockbuster exhibitions, and even large museums like the Metropolitan Museum of Art are beginning to resemble one night, not at the opera, but one night at the television set.

RS: Yes, that's true. What interests me about television as a medium is its fear of boring the audience. Television's philosophy is that things are not supposed to be boring. The way to hold the interest of the audience is to create programming in which events move rapidly forward in a sequence. Most talk shows make for bad television in that nothing happens. The problem, of course, isn't really television but the audience's expectations: we want television to relieve us from tedium. However, boredom is an incredibly important experience for people. It is one of the ways we learn to work, by learning how to get bored with a task. It's one of the ways we learn to love, by learning how to be bored with another human being. Television is a medium that doesn't allow boredom to happen. I think you can make good television, but the culture doesn't want it.

CD: But on public television boredom, in the positive sense, is permissible.

Façade of the Metropolitan Museum, New York. The museum's alignment with American foreign politics and mass entertainment is legitimized in the context of its classical façade.

RS: Yes, and it often succeeds very well! But, as you know, in the United States public television is collapsing. It's becoming more and more popular, and fewer serious programs are getting produced. The funding is disappearing, because the programming is boring. Public television shows long programs about, for example, natural history, which interests me very much. I like to watch little eagles, for instance. But the public says it just isn't interesting, these little birds moving around. The public can't stand the tedium.

CD: How can a museum demonstrate or have the public participate in the experience of boredom?

RS: Maybe we have to show more bad art mixed in with the good. If we agree that museums should be more active, perhaps they must take the risk of boredom as well. Perhaps these two notions that seem so contradictory are in fact opposite sides of the same coin.

"The Artist's Eye," exhibition curated by Francis Bacon, National Gallery, London, 1985. One of the rare occasions when exhibition making is relinquished to an artist as the exhibition's creator.

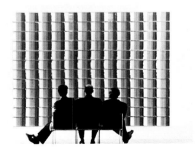

General Idea, Test Pattern: General Idea's TV Dinner Plates (detail), installation at the Spiral Gallery, Tokyo, 1988. Since 1968, the collective General Idea has been working with themes related to the organization of museums.

Projection of sequence of The Rise to Power of Louis XIV by Roberto Rossellini (1964) for Dan Graham's Cinema-Theater during installation at P.S. 1 Museum.

"Theatergarden Bestiarium," P.S. 1 Museum, New York, January 1989. Bottom center: Hermann Pitz, Waterdrops; top left: Dan Graham, Cinema-Theater; left: Jeff Wall, Loge Theater; center: James Coleman, Valor Impositus; right: Rodney Graham, Maritime Theater and Staircase; far right: Bernard Bazile, Antiphonary; top left: Christian-Philipp Müller, Toward a Beltwalk; top right: Christian-Philipp Müller, Cinema Seats Dedicated to R.S.

# THEATERGARDEN BESTIARIUM

## A Brief Guide to the Works in the Exhibition

*Chris Dercon*
*Portfolio by David Levinthal*

From the beginning, "Theatergarden Bestiarium" has been an exhibition in progress. The artists conceived their works and shaped their designs within the framework of Rüdiger Schöttle's text, and the limitations of the design of Schöttle's imaginary garden and the exhibition space. As a result, their works reflect the tension between the autonomy of the artist and the integration of a group show. The artists' works are to be considered "models," meant to test the idea of the exhibition and of the garden.

The entrance to the garden is formed by *Scala* (*Staircase*) by Fortuyn/ O'Brien. It is a gateway built of transparent plates, superimposed over each other, revealing garden elements and theater architecture. Their gateway is conceived of as a scenic theater that refers to the layout of a garden.

The main axis of the "Theatergarden" extends from east to west, meeting the north–south axis at a theater, the *Loge Theater with Its Plan Displayed as an Illuminated Sign* by Jeff Wall. Wall's work is in the shape of a collapsed office building. "The concept of the loge theater of the Baroque," says Wall, "embodies the historical moment of transition from court culture to systematic bureaucratic rule."

The loge originally was a mirrored box in the theater, used by the king, and located directly opposite the center of the stage. The boxes on either side were places to conduct business. In Wall's work, the theater is a lamp, reflecting the monistic orientation of political consolidation that the basic plan of the loge theater represents.

Adjacent to the *Loge Theater* is *Cinema Theater*, by Dan Graham. Graham's work is a movie theater with a glass façade, attached to a "green theater" in a geometric garden, such as the ones at Versailles. A sequence from the film *The Rise to Power of Louis XIV*, directed by Roberto Rossellini and made in 1964, runs continuously in Graham's theater. In the sequence, Rossellini shows the king as an author, director, and main actor in a continuous theatrical work of fiction, staged to consolidate his power.

Below the *Loge Theater* is *Cabbage Without Roots*, by Alain Sechas. Cabbage leaves made of leather evoke a "knot garden." Cabbages, as noted on botanical labels in the kitchen garden at Villandry, near Nantes, France, symbolize happiness and prosperity. The arrangement of Sechas's leaves represents the unified collective in action and in thought. However, for medieval alchemists the sulfur in the plant also represented egoism and false pride.

"As the grounds of the theatergarden slope upward, the mountain range

*"Theatergarden Bestiarium," Casino de la Exposicion, Seville, June 1989. Dan Graham,* Cinema-Theater *(second version: the lights are on in the cinema; there is no projection).*

*Dan Graham presenting his project for "Theatergarden Bestiarium," in Münster, June 1987; next to Dan Graham, from left to right: Jeff Wall, Rüdiger Schöttle, and Rodney Graham.*

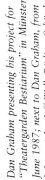

*P.S. 1 Museum. Bottom; Hermann Pitz,* Waterdrops; *left: Alain Sechas,* Cabbage Without Roots; *top center: Fortuyn/ O'Brien,* Scala; *right: Jeff Wall,* Loge Theater; *top right: Dan Graham,* Cinema-Theater.

begins with small shrubbery and bushes," writes Schöttle. Located in the corresponding section of the garden exhibition is Christian-Philipp Müller's *Toward a Beltwalk.* Invented in the second half of the eighteenth century by Capability Brown for use in the English landscape garden, the beltwalk is a walkway leading through a group of landscape and architectural features, intended to enlighten the visitor.

Müller's work shows a cluster of succulents grouped together as in a florist's window display. The second work by Müller, *Cinema Seats Dedicated to R.S.,* takes the form of a rocky landscape, and refers to Robert Smithson's *Toward the Development of a Cinema Cavern (The Moviegoer as a Spelunker)* of 1971. Müller's piece is composed of white chalkstone, purchased for Smithson by the John Weber Gallery in New York.

Behind this "mountain range," Schöttle envisioned an separate enclosure, in which a collage of museum, book, film, and television images were to be projected onto a landscape made of gravel and white chalkstone and reflected in a series of mirrors. With his installation, Schöttle refers to the art cabinet, the grotto, the loge theater, and the hall of mirrors at Amalienburg Pavilion, in the French garden of the Nymphenburg Palace at Munich.

Composer Glenn Branca's musical score, entitled *Bestiarium,* emphasizes the theatrical and cinematic dynamics of the projected slides.

Facing Schöttle's enclosure or grotto, Juan Muñoz constructs a stage on which he sets a prompter's box with a casting of a dwarf. *The Prompter* evokes the theater of memory and the role played by the dwarf in the social and political life of the court culture during the Baroque period, when the dwarf was both accomplice and adversary of the sovereign.

Marin Kasimir, too, connects the ideas of the garden with the ideas of theater and politics. In the theater after the French Revolution, the sovereign was no longer seated in the box opposite the center of the stage, but at the "garden view," to the right of the theater, closer to the stage. The civilian ruler(s) sat on the opposite side and had the "courtyard view." In *Garden View—the Waterfall—Courtyard View,* Kasimir combines the shape of a bench, representing a garden or public space, with a viewing stand, that represents a theater or other architecture designed for the spectacle. The mirrors dividing Kasimir's bench-reviewing stand can be seen as a waterfall flowing into a reflecting lake.

Historically, fountains, ponds, and streams were not only used for decorative purposes, they were also used as light sources with which to further illuminate

particular points of the garden during the day or at night. On one side of Kasimir's lake, Hermann Pitz places transparent pebbles, suggesting the ponds in Japanese gardens. Pitz's piece, *Waterdrops*, can also be understood as a magnifying glass that produces a scientific or photographic image.

On the other side of the lake, Rodney Graham created *Maritime Theater and Staircase*. His monumental stairs or seats evoke the spatial marvel of Baroque architecture, creating the shape of a belvedere and a garden staircase with a positive–negative alternation of a circular form. The architecture itself becomes the show, just like Bramante's stairs in the Exedra of the 1504 Belvedere Courtyard at the Vatican.

James Coleman's *Valor Impositus (Imposed Value)* is an empty museum display case with a disarticulated, half-skeleton, meant for use by students and scholars, lying outside the case. As Coleman himself writes: "The lighting design creates the effect of a display case lit for an exhibition which is not there." Coleman's work underscores the theater of the museum as a theater of representation. As his title indicates, he points to the structure of power. Which is model? Which is viewer? Which is object? And which is subject?

The garden is surrounded by a wall on which Ludger Gerdes projects slides showing the Baroque garden at Schwetzingen near Heidelberg—designed in the second half of the eighteenth century. These slides are intermingled with images of a contemporary garden, *The Valley*, that German artist Erwin Wortelkamp built for himself at Hasselbach, near Bonn. This series is juxtaposed with slides of humorous scenes and remarks about art and life.

Next to Gerdes's projection tower stands the *Antiphonary* by Bernard Bazile. An antiphonary, originally a book of religious chants, was often placed in a pulpit. A choir, divided into two sections, would alternate singing the chants or antiphons. In Bazile's work, the chants are replaced with carpet samples, alluding to the conversations between the organizers, the artists, and the works in the exhibition, as well as to the design of conventional exhibitions and exhibition spaces.

*P.S. 1 Museum. Left: Christian-Philipp Müller,* Toward a Beltwalk; *middle: James Coleman,* Valor Impositus; *background: Juan Muñoz,* The Prompter.

*Juan Muñoz,* The Prompter, *during installation at P.S. 1 Museum.*

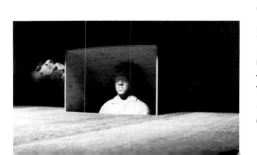

*Casino de la Exposicion. Juan Muñoz,* The Prompter *(second version); background: Christian-Philipp Müller,* Cinema Seats Dedicated to R.S.

*"Theatergarden Bestiarium," Confort Moderne, Poitiers, France, September 1989. Foreground: Hermann Pitz, Waterdrops; middle: Christian-Philipp Müller, Toward a Beltwalk; background: Christian-Philipp Müller, Cinema Seats Dedicated to R.S.*

*P.S. 1 Museum. Left: Rodney Graham,*
Maritime Theater and Staircase; *center:*
*Ludger Gerdes, slide projections; right:*
*Bernard Bazile,* Antiphonary.

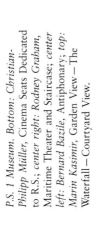

*P.S. 1 Museum. Bottom: Christian-*
*Philipp Müller, Cinema Seats Dedicated*
*to R.S.; center right: Rodney Graham,*
Maritime Theater and Staircase; *center*
*left: Bernard Bazile,* Antiphonary; *top:*
*Marin Kasimir, Garden View —The*
*Waterfall — Courtyard View.*

*Christian-Philipp Müller,* Toward a
Beltwalk *(second version), during*
*installation at Casino de la Exposicion.*

## LIST OF WORKS IN THE EXHIBITION

BERNARD BAZILE
*Antiphonary*, 1989
aluminum, carpet, snakeskin
80cm × 60cm × 120cm

GLENN BRANCA
*Bestiarium*, 1989
9-minute audio recording

JAMES COLEMAN
*Valor Impositus*, 1989
skeleton, glass case
198cm × 130cm × 92cm

FORTUYN/O'BRIEN
*Scala*, 1989
plexiglass, silk, paint
90cm × 190cm × 80cm

LUDGER GERDES
*Untitled*, 1989
243 35mm slides, seven slide projectors,
    wood

DAN GRAHAM
*Cinema Theater*, 1989
(executed by Robin Hurst and Hans
    Sonneveld)
film, projector, plexiglass, mylar, wood
120cm × 200cm × 60cm

RODNEY GRAHAM
*Maritime Theater Staircase*, 1989
wood, metal, styrofoam, paint
100cm diameter × 40 cm

MARIN KASIMIR
*Garden View—The Waterfall—Courtyard
    View*, 1989
wood, paint, mirror
200cm × 200cm × 80cm

JUAN MUÑOZ
*The Prompter*, 1989
papier-mâché, paint, wood
100cm × 80cm × 60cm

CHRISTIAN-PHILIPP MÜLLER
*Toward a Beltwalk*, 1989
plants, leather, aluminum
90cm × 150cm × 90cm

CHRISTIAN-PHILIPP MÜLLER
*Cinema Seats Dedicated to R.S.*, 1989
chalkstone
90cm × 150cm × 90cm

HERMANN PITZ
*Waterdrops*, 1989
acrylic
250cm × 350cm × 20cm

ALAIN SECHAS
*Cabbage Without Roots*, 1989
leather, metal
120cm × 120cm × 40cm

RÜDIGER SCHÖTTLE
*Untitled*, 1989
597 35mm slides, seven projectors, sand,
    gravel, chalkstone, mirror

JEFF WALL
*Loge Theater With Its Plan Displayed as an
    Illuminated Sign*, 1989
polyester, paint, lights on wooden base
60cm × 60cm × 80cm

*P.S. 1 Museum. Rüdiger Schöttle, slide
projections.*

Portfolio by David Leventhal of "Theatergarden Bestiarium," at P.S. 1 Museum, January–March 1989.

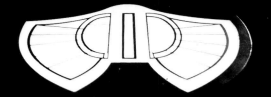

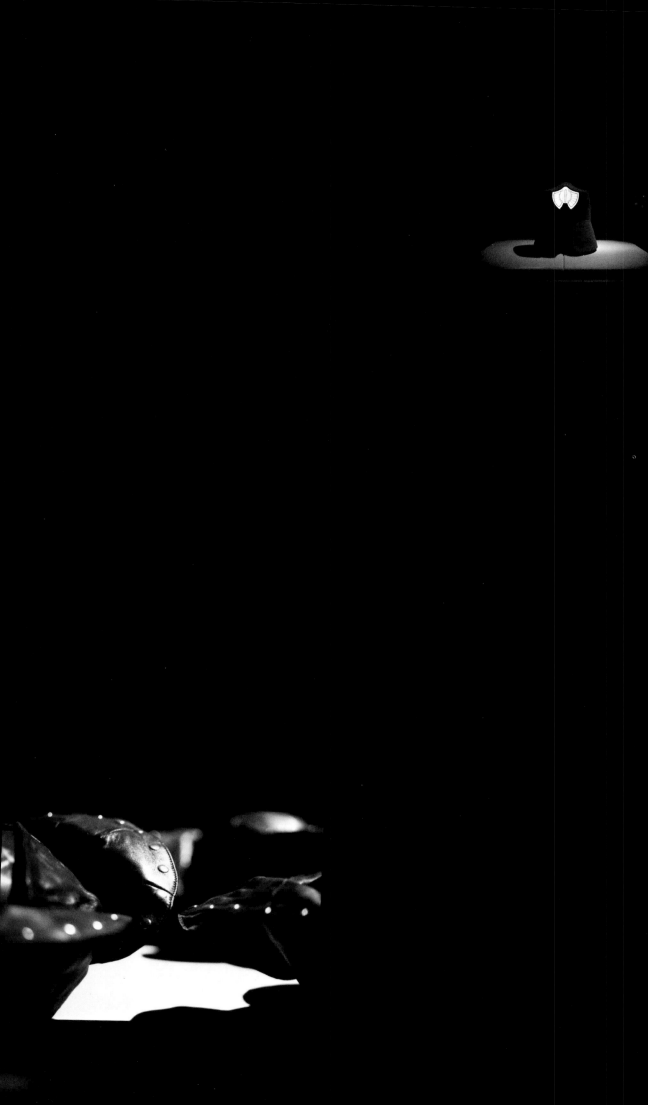

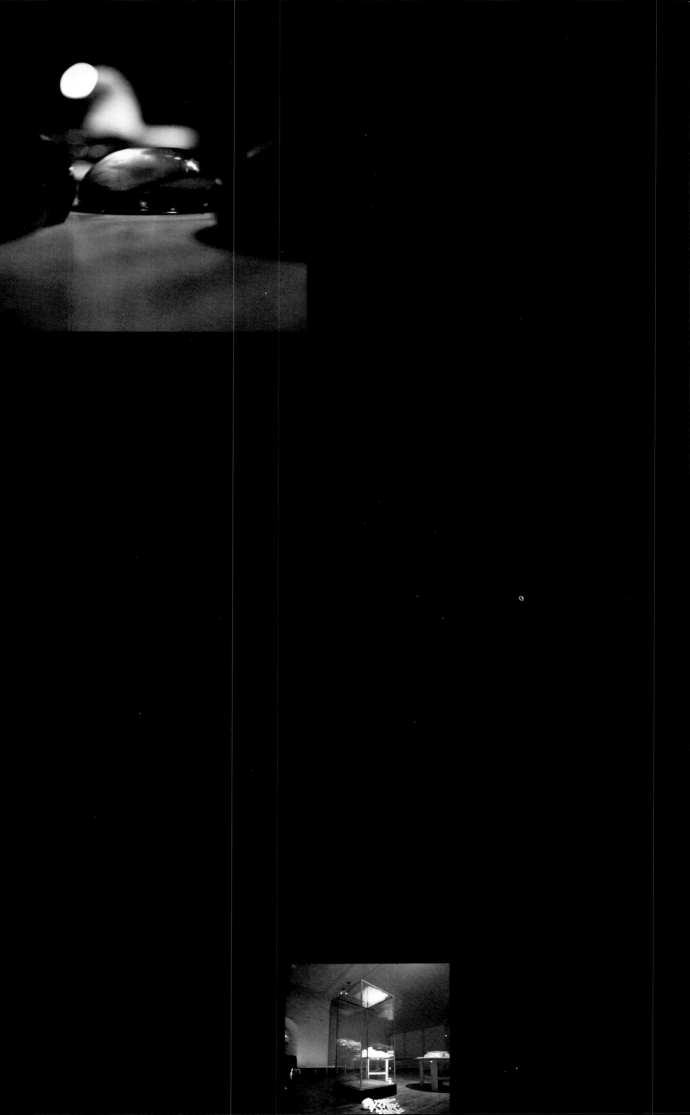

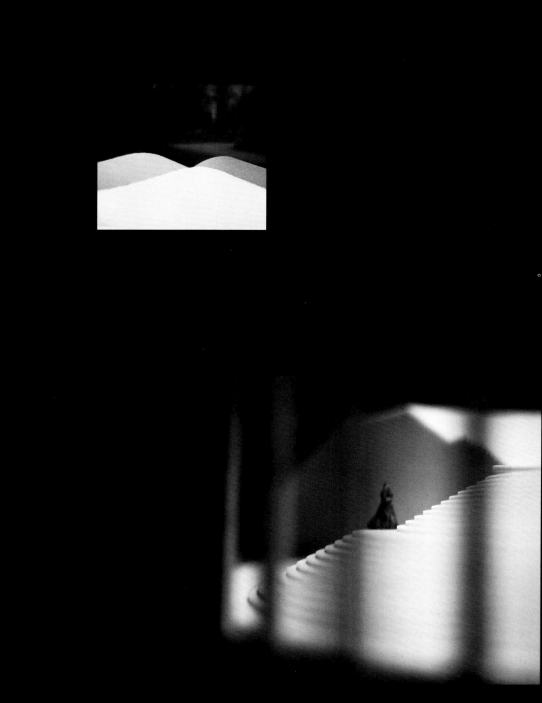

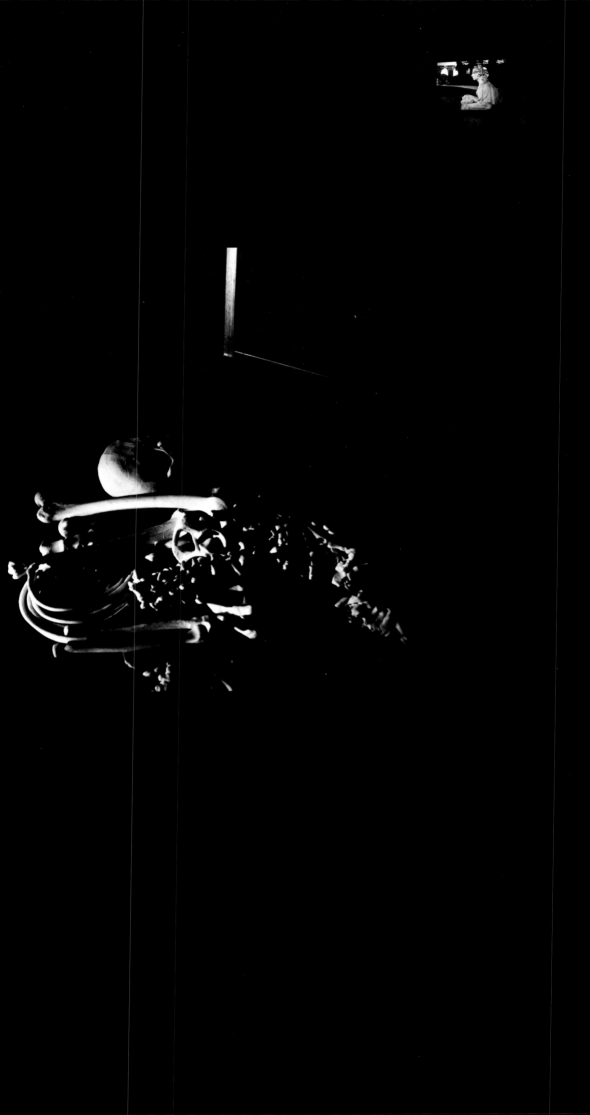

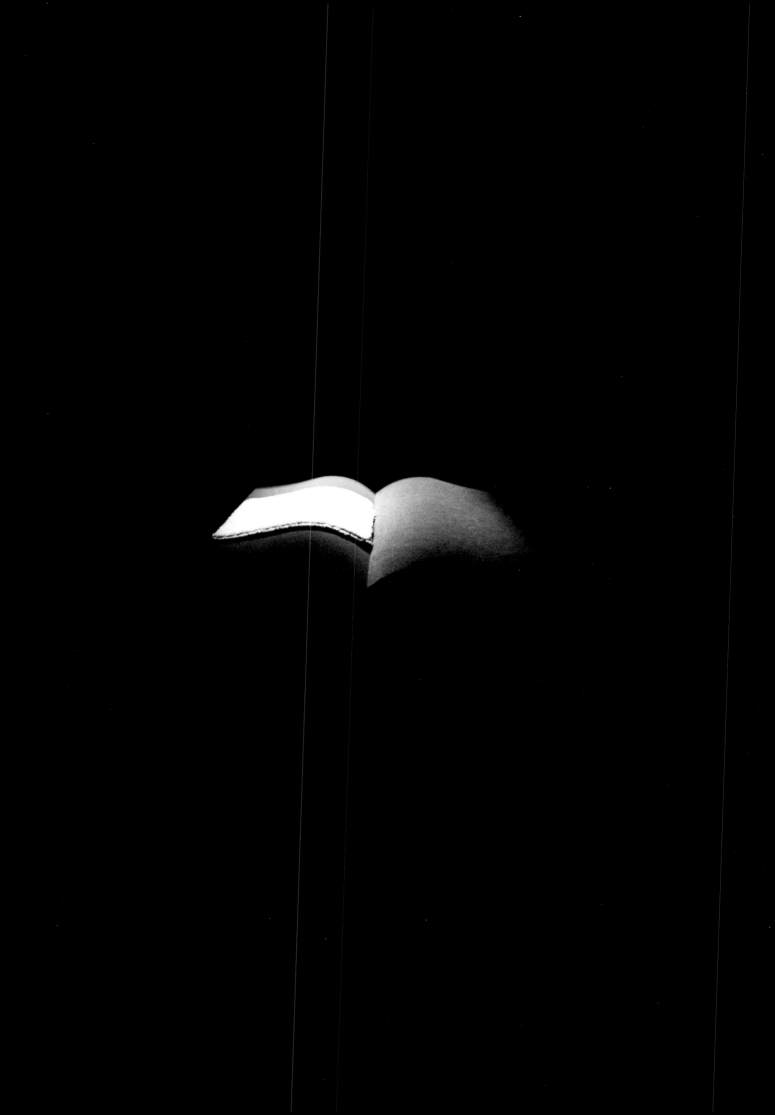

# Texts Without a Grave

*Marianne Brouwer*

### Prologue

After an absence of many years I came back to the city of T. where I once lived.

The city was known for the fact that its inhabitants were constantly changing its buildings, streets, even entire neighborhoods, replacing them almost overnight.

Nothing remained as I had known it. The street where my house had been had disappeared as well. When, after hours of wandering on a hot afternoon, I finally discovered its former location, I was amazed to find that, although the houses had disappeared and the street itself had been rebuilt, the shadows remained.

I know the city like an Indian knows his landscape—from the smallest crack in the pavement to the color of a lintel—in fragments connected to events.

We stalk through the city like hunters on guard, dodging and hiding or springing from ambush. And in all the stone, asphalt, and walls is meaning, sucked up by the pores of the bricks, reflected by windows, shaped by the gates, whispered by trees, defended by walls, are memories. But the sound of the city is a vast roar—all languages at once, screeching, crying, and whistling like the sound of the ocean, which is the sound of your own blood when you put a seashell to your ear.

With every step, I remember. Walking now, I remember by the sinews of my feet. The sights that my eyes have forgotten are yielded to me by shadows of long vanished things. Although my body knows about aging, it does not know time. There is no apparent distance between forgetting and the sudden remembrance of what has been forgotten. Not a single instant seems to have passed. And yet this is an irrevocable moment. To remember is the final death of what has been forgotten.

### Mnemosyne

The detective story, the story of intimate crime, is almost a century older than the cinema. Yet it seems as if their origins are deeply rooted in identical phenomena.

At a press conference Jean-Luc Godard gave in Cannes for his film *Passion*, he described the origins of screenwriting:

*The script was invented by bookkeepers who had to keep an account of what Mack Sennett had to shoot each day. So they drew up a list: a pair of stockings, a car, a policeman, a girl, a bathing suit. . . . Later on they added verbs and adjectives: a girl in a bathing suit loves a policeman who drives three cars. And this was called a movie script.*

In the beginning was the object—the bookkeeper's random props—which, when strung together with the right verbs and adjectives, are the clues to a narrative that at the same time absorbs them. The first analytical detective story in history, "The Murders in the Rue Morgue" by Edgar Allan Poe, begins with a similar inventory—a still life as unfrivolous as it is seemingly random:

*. . . On the hearth were two or three long and thick tresses of grey human hair, also dabbled with blood, and seeming to have been pulled out by the roots. Upon the floor were found four Napoleons, an earring of topaz, three large silver spoons, three smaller of métal d'alger, and two bags, containing nearly four thousand francs in gold.*

It is the task of the detective not only to eliminate the *wrong* objects but even more to insert the *right* verbs and adjectives, until the coherent narrative, the *right* script, emerges in an analytical flash.

The perpetrator of the crime and the author of the script are necessarily one and the same person. His identity is (re)constructed from those random clues he unconsciously leaves behind. The clues point to the perpetrator in the same way as objects point out their subject. Through the object, the subject meets its destiny.

In the cinema, such objects are projected as a continuous collage, creating images without shadow or substance, the images of a luminous and translucent dream. Meaning falls away; it, too, becomes transparent, as the spectator is absorbed into the pictures the projector casts on the wall before him. These pictures, originating from darkness, seem to originate from *his* mind. He is the secret author of the narrative that unfolds before his eyes. Yet the story of the (re)construction is itself not enough to create the suspense that glues us to our seats. In the detective story, suspense has a moral quality. Between the detective and the criminal, between author and the other, there is a relationship as if they were lovers.

The detective is the only person able to evoke the image of his adversary and bring it to life, because his mind identifies so thoroughly as to become his double. And who knows whether, from the very beginning, the criminal does not long for the detective to discover him, thus affirming his existence? It is as if underneath the coherent surface of the tale of crime and punishment there is an undercurrent of another story.

An ancient drama, which has lost its coherence, of which there are only relics—objects that were images once. Superficially, the detective story restores order to a disordered and frightened society; yet its very existence evokes something quite different. For who can tell whether the two authors are not really one and the same

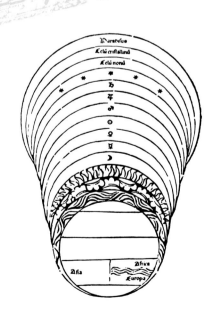

*The spheres of the universe as a memory system, in Jacobus Publicius, Oratoriae artis epitome, Venice, 1482.*

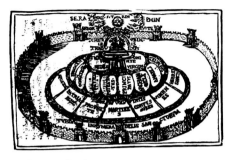

person—whether guilt or innocence do not exclusively depend on the way the clues are initially constructed?

These are the landscapes of the mind—a strangely realistic, yet visionary horror—spaces that seem to be totally interior, without any visible connection to a given, outside world. In this limbo, in which time seems suspended, the symbolic still exists, but its language has fallen apart and become a "forest of signs" (Rainer Maria Rilke). A steady, yet sourceless light shines in these regions, coming from nowhere but penetrating everywhere. Through these spaces, which have no beginning, no end, no center, which are filled with the great ruins of ancient eras, human beings wander like bodiless shadows. Their movements are dictated by the need to find some kind of meaning, some kind of existence. But all that meets them is silence. The monuments of old no longer speak; they exist only as fragments—fragments that can no longer signify. Instruments of torture, they are bathed in an eternal twilight, in which there is neither night nor day, heaven nor hell. Everything is memory; everything speaks of memory, but what offers itself is not memory but its fragmented signs.

*Hell as artificial memory, in Cosmos Rossellius,* Thesaurus Artificiosae Memoriae, *Venice, 1579.*

*Paradise as artificial memory, in Cosmos Rossellius,* Thesaurus Artificiosae Memoriae, *Venice, 1579.*

## READING THE CITY

There is a city in India whose ground plan is the image of Kali, the goddess of fertility and destruction. Each curved street follows a part of her divine body. Temples have been built on all her chakras, and another one, the most important, stands above her navel, in the middle of the body of the god Shiva whom she carries in her womb.

The city of Beijing, and, after its example, all ancient cities in China and Japan, was based on the figure of the square, the streets forming a grid. Along the streets, the temples and gates are arranged to form a strict symmetrical hierarchy. The innermost squares contain the palace of the emperor, whom no commoner was permitted to look at on pain of death. The numbers used in construction were three, five, nine—the heavenly numbers; seven—heaven and earth combined; and eight—the earth. The Chinese saw the city as belonging to the earth, represented by the square, which is both manifold and finite, while the heaven was circular, unending, and perfect in itself.

The essential image of the city of the Renaissance is contained in the *Theater of the World,* invented by the philosopher Giulio Camillo in the mid-sixteenth century. This portable, wooden structure was shaped like a circular amphitheater, consisting of "seven times seven gates, on seven rising grades." In its center one person could sit. On its wall were inscribed all the signs and symbols of the Christian Renaissance: the stars, the planets, the Greek gods and their attributes, animals and plants, the elements and their alchemical symbols, the temperaments, the vices, and the virtues. The theater also contained wooden drawers, filled with written texts that combined all those elements into a "universal book."

*For you must know that it is by one and the same ladder that nature descends to the production of things and the intellect ascends to the knowledge of them; and that the one and the other proceeds from unity and returns to unity, passing through the multitude of things in the middle.*
Bruno Giordano de la Causa, quoted in F. A. Yates, *The Art of Memory*

Every city contains its own symbolism, its own "Città Ideale" as its implicit goal, connecting the topology and the symbolic. It links heaven and earth as well as east and west, finite and infinite, visible and invisible.

The layout of the city is a huge ideogram, allowing the spectator to grasp the entire cosmology it represents, while at the same time, he is aware that each one of his movements is part of that design. Not limited to the city alone, coding and decoding are equally applicable to books and paintings, diagrams and maps, systems of fortunetelling or magic, numerology or alphabets.

Anyone who knows the codes is able to decipher their intrinsic meanings, for they are all of an ideogrammatic nature, functioning as clues to memory. Each of them embodies the art of Mnemosyne, the visual aid to memorizing the universe that they represent; or, perhaps, it would be better to say the universe that they *present* because they *are* that universe. Without their material presence, the universe would remain invisible, and no power could be derived from it. These are systems based on the principle of physical reciprocity and not, like metaphysics, on the denial of matter.

The codes determine history as well as the people who live in them. They determine language as well as those that speak it, from the highest to the lowest class, assigning each its proper place.

There are, however, two exceptions: the King and the Outlaw, who are both exempt from the symbolic. Placed at the highest and lowest extremes of the system, representing Good and Evil, Heaven and Hell, they themselves are outside representation: the Outlaw because he has no name, no place, not even a grave; the King because his is the ideal image for all to see. Yet, he can only fulfill his role for others. He cannot represent himself. The place of both is truly atopos, the nonplace into which all meanings converge and are absorbed.

Out of the closed universe of the symbolic city, the universally open Metropolis arose, offering the images of unbounded freedom, endless possibility, unlimited production to each and everyone.

The Metropolis thus became the metaphor for desire and ecstasy, a modern Paradise promising eternal life and never-ending happiness in an endless day.

The image of the city evolved into the image of a stream, a constant flow of people and goods, circulating through immense arteries of traffic, aligned with the signs of the new age: banks, railroad stations, monuments, and department stores.

Its horizontal structure connotes time (speed and progress); its vertical structure connotes power (social hierarchy). Its spaces are no longer determined by proportion and measure, but they arrange themselves in a concentration of separate signs. Each building, each object, each human being seems part of a cinematic collage endlessly unwinding in a space without depth.

The language of the city is the mechanistic language of modern, medical science. In this terminology the body is the simile for the city. The higher, or upper, parts of the city-body are synonymous with hygiene; that is, with sunlight, fresh air, and open spaces—with a healthy mind in a healthy body, wealth, power, and all the desirable things they bring.

The lower regions of the urban body are located in the sewers. Their language, their population represent the intolerable, the anal, the sexual, the outcast, put underground and out of sight. In its terminology, poverty, sin, and crime are called diseases. Vermin stand for beggars, whores, criminals, Jews, or Gypsies. The appropriate terms associated with them are sanitation and extermination.

Thus, the Metropolis simultaneously presents a realm of man's infinite desire, the "Ideal," as well as the highly controlling language systems of official, political power.

The Metropolis encloses a memory system at least as powerful as those of ancient cities. But whereas the latter originated in the Ideal, from heaven as embodied in and reflected by their symbolic layout, the modern city presents its ideal image in order to stimulate desire and to forget, to cover-up and mask repression.

All these signs evoke images of life, of production as the negation of death, of history as the road of development and progress. Yet each torn-down building,

*Calcutta, 1887–94.*

each sanitized street contains the unspoken and unspeakable language of shadows, the memory of that which it represses.

Within these realms, within the Age of Liberty, every man, King or Outlaw, rules no one but himself. He is his own supreme subject, the center of representation, into which all meanings converge and are absorbed. All around him, he gathers the signs that point him out as his own author, his "self," the subject of the narrative that proves his existence. Yet, he himself is excluded from representation. His very self is atopos, nonplace. But who shall decide whether he has created this panorama, whose center he imagines himself to be, or whether this panorama has created him?

*But there was no voice throughout the vast illimitable desert,*
*And the characters upon the rock were SILENCE.*
Edgar Allan Poe, "Silence—a Fable"

Constructing one's own identity from the aleatory or random objects that offer themselves to the longing gaze is the heroic, melancholy tale of bourgeois society.

From Edgar Allan Poe to August Strindberg and Stéphane Mallarmé, to Franz Kafka and the Surrealists, there has been an urge to code and decode human fate by the gathering and reading of signs.

The Metropolis is the encompassing register, the universal book, in which every chance encounter is a cipher of a secret destiny that is gradually revealed by discontinuous and accidental meetings. When Strindberg wanders obsessively through the streets of Paris, he interprets every street name, the number of houses, each inscription and chance encounter in cabalistic terms, as if the city were one enormous anagram revealing to him, not eternal life and happiness, but spelling out Inferno and madness. For everything appears as a shadow of a language that can no longer signify, or in which all signifiers have come to mean the same.

In Mallarmé's "A Throw of Dice" it is finally language itself that forms an anagram of ciphers that can be read both horizontally and vertically, as well as in any combination:

*. . . not the voices of any one being,*
*But of a multitude of beings,*

*And, varying in their cadences from syllable to syllable,*
*Fell duskily upon our ears*
*In the well remembered and familiar accents*
*Of many thousand departed friends.*
Edgar Allan Poe, "Shadow—a Parable"

These are the voices of the shadows that produce themselves within a syntax from which the subject is dropped, the subject that speaks and writes: I think, I am— without a future or a past, without a history, for there can be no history, this body machine keeps screaming and screaming in order to release what cannot and must not be said.

      It is the black hole, disgorging what it has sucked up. There is no image to redeem its memory, no sign in which to confront it with itself.

## THE EVIDENCE: THE ARCHIVES

*The silence of the sirens is more dangerous than their song.*
Franco Rella, "Il Silenzio e le Parole"

      Nothing shall remain hidden; everything is to be accessible to history. So let me attempt to track down history in its remains, which are stored in the huge cardboard boxes that have been placed on my desk. What did this city used to look like?

      There are the photo albums, although few. There are also many small piles of photos neatly pasted on cardboard, arranged according to street names.

      These photos show tip carts driving along tracks through the ruins of the same streets that now, in this new age, look as if they were built from a special kind of cardboard.

      These photographs are dated from 1947, and according to their inscriptions they were taken by a professional photographer commissioned by the city. Men and women in dark overcoats, stepping through caved-in doorways and passing along high, neatly arranged piles of bricks, bicycle or walk to work in a quiet, orderly fashion.

      The photo albums show snapshots of devastated houses with captions that tell that these were the homes of friends and neighbors. There is a photo of an exploding bomb that looks like fireworks. A farmer has photographed his shoe next

*Memory system, in Giordano Bruno, De umbris idearum, Paris, 1582.*

to a bomb crater in his potato field to indicate their relative sizes. Pasted in one of the albums is a poem printed in Gothic script, a prayer for the crushing of the enemy.

Other photographs show canals that have caved in on top of ships, façades torn from houses to reveal a heartbreaking variety of period wallpapers, closets burst open, beds hanging upside down through collapsed ceilings.

Then there is a special pile of albums—special because the snapshots appear to have been taken systematically. The inscription on the cover indicates that these albums were donated to the archives by a police inspector. It must have been his job to supervise and organize the evacuation of the wounded, to have the dead carried away, the fires extinguished, the survivors calmed.

These are uncanny photographs. For where are they, these people, where have they gone in between the moment of disaster and the moment when this official, who obviously was an amateur photographer who captured history in the guise of the destroyed dentist's office, the burnt-out cathedral, and so many houses, from which smoke often still rises? There is no human that animates these absurd and grotesque still lifes.

There is the occasional photograph of soldiers crowding into their vehicles after the job has been done. And there are photos the photographer seems to have enjoyed taking, of a jumping contest for police horses, of his men being decorated. But there is nothing, nothing at all to show his feelings, feelings he must have had about the horrors he witnessed, to which he became a witness when he set himself the task of capturing history in photographs he ultimately donated to the archives.

It is as if, in the interval between the catastrophe of the war and the moment the traffic was able to start again, something happened, something had to happen. An instant of deconstruction, of an intense denial of loss. For none of these photographs shows a single second of perplexity, of indignation, not a trace of a hesitating hand, not a stain of a tear.

In the air-conditioned, neon-lit environment of the archives, these cartons store another kind of death. For nothing speaks. Everything is silence.

*To fill a Gap*
*Insert the thing that caused it—*
*Block it up with Other*
*And 'twill yawn the more—*
*you cannot solder an Abyss*
*with Air.*

*There is a pain so utter*
*It swallows substance up—*
*Then covers the Abyss*
*With trance*
*So memory can step*
*Around—Across—Upon it*
Emily Dickinson

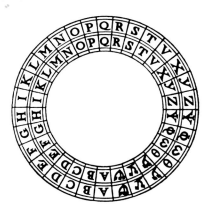

*Memory wheels, in Giordano Bruno, De umbris idearum, Paris, 1582.*

*Calcutta, 1887–94.*

## RÜDIGER SCHÖTTLE

Rüdiger Schöttle was born in Stuttgart in 1941. He lives in Munich. Schöttle has curated exhibitions including "Austellung B" (Munich, 1982); "Laputa" (Stuttgart, 1983); "Idea" (Stuttgart, 1984); "Louis XIV Tanzt" (Munich, 1985, and Zurich, 1986); theatrical productions including *Beggars Follies* at the Tanz-Film and Musikfestival (Munich, 1985). He has also created a series of slide shows, including *Res Publica* at the "Von Hier Aus" exhibition (Düsseldorf, 1984). In 1988, Schöttle exhibited an installation *Wool and Water* at the Victoria Miro Gallery (London).

## BERNARD BAZILE

Born in Tulle, France, in 1952. Lives in Paris. Bernard Bazile worked with Jean-Marc Bustamante from 1982–87 under the name BazileBustamante. In 1988, they began to work separately. Exhibitions include "Sonsbeek '86" (Arnheim, Holland, 1986) and "A Distanced View," The New Museum (New York, 1986).

## GLENN BRANCA

Born in Harrisburg, Pennsylvania, in 1948. Lives in New York City. Glenn Branca's performances and orchestrations of mainstream rock music have been used by numerous dance and theater companies, filmmakers, and performance artists, including the Alvin Ailey Company, The Twyla Tharp Company, Peter Greenaway, and Robert Longo. Performances in collaboration with visual artists include Dan Graham, Kunsthalle (Bern, 1983), and Rüdiger Schöttle, "Louis XIV Tanzt" (Munich, 1985).

## JAMES COLEMAN

Born in Ballaghadreen, County Roscommon, Ireland, in 1941. Lives in Dublin. Exhibitions have been held at The Renaissance Society (Chicago, 1985), Marian Goodman Gallery (New York, 1987), Artists Space (New York, 1988).

## FORTUYN/O'BRIEN

Irene Fortuyn was born in Geldrop, Netherlands, in 1959 and lives in Amsterdam. Robert O'Brien was born in Bromyard, Great Britain, in 1951. He died in Amsterdam in April 1988. Fortuyn/O'Brien began their collaboration in 1983. Exhibitions include "View over the Ocean, Part II," Artists Space (New York, 1984); "Sonsbeek '86" (Arnheim, Netherlands, 1986); "A Distanced View," The New Museum (New York, 1986).

## LUDGER GERDES

Born in Lastrup, West Germany, in 1954. Lives in Düsseldorf and Munich. Exhibitions include "Konstruierte Orte," Kunsthalle (Bern, 1983); "The European Iceberg—Creativity in Germany and Italy Today," Art Gallery of Toronto, 1985; "Skulpturen Projekte" (Münster, 1987).

## DAN GRAHAM

Born in Urbana, Illinois, in 1942. Lives in New York City. Exhibitions include "Sonsbeek '86" (Arnheim, Netherlands, 1986); "Skulpturen Projekte" (Münster, 1987); Marian Goodman Gallery (New York, 1987); "New Urban Landscape" (New York, 1988).

## RODNEY GRAHAM

Born in Vancouver, British Columbia, in 1948. Lives in Vancouver. Exhibitions include "Skulpturen Projekte" (Münster, 1987); Christine Burgin Gallery (New York, 1988).

## MARIN KASIMIR

Born in Munich in 1957. Lives in Brussels. Exhibitions have been held at Galerie Joost Declercq (Ghent, Belgium, 1987); Kunststichting Kanaal (Kortrijk, Belgium, 1988); Palais des Beaux Arts (Charleroi, Belgium, 1988).

## CHRISTIAN-PHILIPP MÜLLER

Born in Bienne, Switzerland, in 1957. Lives in Brussels. Exhibitions include "Carl Theodor's Garten" (Hellerhof, Düsseldorf, 1987); "Eh! Bien Prenons la Plume" in Arti et Amicitiae (Amsterdam, 1988).

JUAN MUÑOZ
Born in Madrid in 1952. Lives in Madrid.
Exhibitions include Stedelijk Van
Abbemuseum (Eindhoven, Netherlands,
1985); "Chambres D'Amis" (Ghent,
Belgium, 1986); "Aperto '86," Venice
Biennale; Konrad Fisher Gallery (Cologne,
1988).

HERMANN PITZ
Born in Oldenburg, West Germany, in 1956.
Lives in Düsseldorf. Exhibitions include
"Skulpturen Projekte" (Münster, 1987);
Christine Burgin Gallery (New York, 1987);
"Berlin Art," Museum of Modern Art (New
York, 1987); Brooklyn Museum (Brooklyn,
New York, 1987); "Aperto '88," Venice
Biennale.

ALAIN SECHAS
Born in 1955. Lives in Paris. Exhibitions
include "Contained Attitudes," Artists
Space (New York, 1986); Galerie Ghislaine
Hussenot (Paris, 1988).

JEFF WALL
Born in Vancouver, British Columbia, in
1946. Lives in Vancouver. Exhibitions
include "Documenta 8" (Kassel, 1987);
"Carnegie International," Carnegie
Museum of Art (Pittsburgh, Pennsylvania,
1988); "Les Magiciens de la Terre," Centre
Georges Pompidou (Paris, 1989).

PAUL ROBBRECHT AND HILDE DAEM
Paul Robbrecht and Hilde Daem are
architects in Ghent. They received acclaim
for their project Architecture for Zeeland
(Middelburg, 1985) and Esplanade
(Rotterdam, 1989). Robbrecht and Daem
have contributed architectural components
to exhibitions in Ghent—"Initiatief 1986"
and in Amsterdam—"Wall for a
Painting/Floor for a Sculpture" (De Appel
Foundation, 1987). They will design
"Documenta 9" (Kassel) in 1992.

MARIANNE BROUWER
Marianne Brouwer studied art history at the
University of Leyden and at the Sorbonne in
Paris. She writes for the Dutch magazine
Museumjournaal and has contributed to
numerous exhibition catalogs including the
catalog for "Skulpturen Projekte" (Münster)
in 1987. Since 1981 she has been curator for
contemporary sculpture at the Rijksmuseum
Kroller-Müller in Otterlo, Netherlands.

ANTJE VON GRAEVENITZ
Antje von Graevenitz teaches art history at
the University of Amsterdam. She has
contributed to numerous exhibition catalogs
in the Netherlands and Germany including
the catalog for "Bilderstreit" (Cologne) in
1989. She is currently the editor of the
Dutch architectural magazine Archis.

JOHANNE LAMOUREUX
Johanne Lamoureux teaches art history at
the universities of Ottawa and Concordia
(Canada). She writes art criticism for the
Canadian magazine Parachute and has also
collaborated on several catalogs and articles
for museums. She is especially interested in
museology and contemporary procedures of
exhibition making.

FRÉDÉRIC MIGAYROU
Frédéric Migayrou studied philosophy at the
Sorbonne in Paris. He has written art
criticism for French magazines including
Artistes, Des Arts, and Public. He has
contributed to exhibition catalogs on James
Coleman, Günther Förg, Dan Graham, and
Jeff Wall. Migayrou is currently the editor of
One Example.

NAOMI MILLER
Naomi Miller teaches art history at Boston
University. She has published many books,
including Renaissance Bologna (1989),
Heavenly Caves: Reflections on the Garden
Grotto (1982), and French Renaissance
Fountains (1977). From 1975 to 1984 she
was book review editor of The Journal of the
Society of Architectural Historians.

RICHARD SENNETT
Richard Sennett is professor of sociology at
New York University, where he also holds
the chair of University Professor of the
Humanities. He has published many books
and articles on urban history, theater, and
social psychology. He is the author of The
Fall of Public Man (1977), Palais Royal
(1987), and Civitas (1989).

The Institute for Contemporary Art is a nonprofit center for contemporary art committed to the presentation of a broad range of artistic activities in various media, through exhibitions, performances, film and video screenings, and related activities.

P.S. 1 Museum and The Clocktower Gallery facilities are owned by the City of New York. Their operations are supported in part by the Department of Cultural Affairs, City of New York.

Richard Bellamy
Nancy Bowditch
Mr. and Mrs. Robert Buxton
Beverly and Daniel Cannold
Patricia and James Cayne
Irwin B. Cohen
Jane and John Comfort
Charles Cowles
Elaine and Werner Dannheisser
Rosie and Ricardo DeAnda
Martha and Guy Demange
Mary M. Denison
Laura Donnelley
William S. Ehrlich
Richard Ekstract
Andre Emmerich
Mathew and Edythe Gladstein
Barbara Gladstone
Sara and Seth Glickenhaus
Marian Goodman
Peter A. Gordon
Edwin Havlovic
Barbara and Donald Jonas
Mr. and Mrs. I.H. Kempner III
Nathan Kolodner
Robert Layton
Ira Levy and Stan Gurell
Vera G. List
Ronay and Richard Menschel
Sue and Eugene Mercy
Enid and Lester Morse
Mr. and Mrs. George C. Muellich
Louis and Mary S. Myers
David Rockefeller
Phillip E. Romero
Jackson S. Ryan, Jr.
Douglas Schoen
Fredrick Sherman
Jerry I. Speyer
Estelle and Harold Tanner
George H. Waterman, III
Anonymous

CONTRIBUTING MEMBERS
David Bermant
Eddo A. Bult
Confort & Co., Inc.
Mr. and Mrs. Kenneth N. Dayton
Mr. and Mrs. James S. DeSilva
Virginia Dwan
Ronald Feldman Fine Arts Inc.
Lawton Wehle Fitt
Mr. & Mrs. Arthur Fleischer
Mr. and Mrs. Arnold C. Forde

Arthur Goldberg
Mr. & Mrs. Ira B. Kapp
Miner S. and Marianne Keeler
Mrs. Robert H. Levi
Sidney and Frances Lewis
Lewis Manilow
Alfredo de Marzio
David McKee Inc.
James I. McLaren
Zachary P. Morfogen
Midori Nishizawa and Akira Ikeda
James G. Pepper
David N. Pincus
Mr. & Mrs. Ned L. Pines
Mikael Salovaara and Beth Allison Stewart
Dan Scheuer
Ileana Sonnabend
Robert G. Wilmers
Anonymous

STAFF
Alanna Heiss, *President and Executive Director*
Gwen Darien, *Deputy Director*
Chris Dercon, *Program Director*
Hank Stahler, *Building Director*
Thomas Finkelpearl, *Clocktower Director*
Rebecca Quaytman, *Program Coordinator*
George York, *Education Director*
Pablo Narvaez, *Technical Coordinator*
Ken Ansley, *Development and Fiscal Assistant*
Audrey Walen, *Executive and Publications Assistant*
David Williams, *Receptionist and Program Assistant*
Tim Noe, *Technical Coordinator*
Marin Paun, *Building Superintendent*
Frederick Cisterna, *Assistant*
Liz French, *Assistant*
Kathy Kao, *Bookkeeper*

Carole Kismaric, *Director of Publications*
Ari Marcopoulos, *Photographer*
Catherine Arthus-Bertrand, *Intern*
Julie Yee, *Publications Intern*

ACKNOWLEDGMENTS
This publication and the exhibition "Theatergarden Bestiarium" would not have been possible without the support, assistance, and cooperation of many people. Major funding has been provided by The National Endowment for the Arts. Additional funding was provided by the governments of Belgium, Canada, France, the Netherlands, Spain, and the city of Zurich; Goethe House, New York; and the International Committee of The Institute for Contemporary Art.
We are grateful to the artists who participated in this project, especially for their graciousness, professionalism, and openness. We are also thankful for Rüdiger Schöttle, whose concept and design provided the impetus for this project.
We are especially grateful to Véronique Dabin, Hans Sonneveld, and Hank Stahler, who supported and worked on this project for more than two years.
Saskia Bos, Hilde Daem, Catherine David, Joshua Decter, Dan Graham, Peter Missotten, Christian-Philipp Müller, Paul Robbrecht, and Jeff Wall provided valuable advice and suggestions.
Thanks to James Acevedo, Nathan Budoff, Mark Curran, Kanani Dower, Jill Entis, Katarina Isaksson, Michael LeCompte, Larry List, Pablo Narvaez, Tim Noe, Ray Sage, Frederick Cisterna, Don Trubey, and Edward J. Vadvarka for building the exhibition.
Gwen Darien, Kevin Power, and Guy Tortosa are to be thanked for their belief in the project.
This publication would not have been possible without the efforts of Carole Kismaric and Susan Jonas in editorial direction; Lawrence Wolfson in design; Audrey Walen and Julie Yee in research and editorial assistance; and Stefaan Decostere, whose film documentaries provided inspiration for the illustrations in this publication. Joachim Neugroschel and Benno Groeneveld prepared lucid translations.

Alanna Heiss
*President and Executive Director*

Chris Dercon
*Program Director*

Unless otherwise noted, credits read from top to bottom and are separated by semi-colons.

BESTIARIUM, THEATER AND GARDEN OF VIOLENCE, WAR, AND HAPPINESS. Pps. 8–13: Rüdiger Schöttle, Munich.
MANY DREAMS OF MANY GARDENS. P. 14: The Museum of Modern Art/Film Stills Archive, New York (2); *3e Schrift,* Arnhemse Academie Pers, Arnhem, 1984; MOMA/Film Stills Archive (background). P. 15: *Heavenly Caves Reflections on the Garden Grotto,* Naomi Miller, George Braziller Inc., New York, 1987; *Encyclopedismo in Roma Barocco, Athanasius Kirchner e il Museo del Collegio Romano, tra Wunderkammer e Museo Scientifico,* Venice, 1986. P. 16: Rüdiger Schöttle; MOMA/Film Stills Archive (2); MOMA, New York, Abbott-Levy Collection, Partial Gift of Shirley C. Burden, New York (background). P. 17: Rüdiger Schöttle (5). P. 18: Hans Sonneveld, Brussels; Marin Kasimir, Brussels; Irene Fortuyn, Amsterdam; Schloss Nymphenburg, Munich (background). P. 19: Paul Robbrecht and Hilde Daem, Ghent (2); MOMA/Film Stills Archive. P. 20: Peter Missotten, Brussels; The National Trust, Essex, England; The Bettmann Archive Inc., New York; *London, 2,000 Years of a City and Its People,* Felix Barker and Peter Jackson, Macmillian Publishing and Co., Inc., New York, 1974 (background). P. 21: Gerd Pfeiffer, Munich; Rodney Graham, Vancouver; *Kunstforum International,* Cologne. P. 22: Christian Philipp-Müller; Manfred Jade, Brussels. Pps. 22–23: Christine Burgin Gallery, New York (background). P. 23: John Weber Gallery, New York; Christine Burgin Gallery; Photograph by Jennifer Kotter, Ronald Feldman Fine Arts Inc., Collection Alan and Cindy Lewin, New York. P. 24: Bettmann (2). P. 25: Garnier Flammarion, Paris. P. 26: Ludger Gerdes, Düsseldorf. P. 27: Centre d'Art Contemporain, Geneva. P. 28: Geoffrey James, Canadian Museum of Contemporary Photography/National Museums of Canada, Musée Canadien de la photographie contemporaine/Musées nationaux du Canada. P. 29: The Walker Art Center, Minneapolis-Gift of Fredrick R. Weissman in honor of his parents, William and Mary Weissman, 1988.
THINKING AHEAD: IDEAS, COMMENTS, AND PROJECTS FOR "THEATERGARDEN BESTIARIUM". Pps. 32–59: All illustrations courtesy of the artists except *El Primo,* collection of Prado, Madrid. Pps. 38–39: Photographs by Attilio Maranzano. P. 42: Models built by Robin Hurst and Hans Sonneveld; Pps. 56–57: Models built by Ewen McNeil and Wayne Smith.
THE STAGE AND THE REGISTER: EVERYTHING IS ARTIFICE IN "THEATERGARDEN BESTIARIUM."
P. 60: Frédéric Migayrou, Paris (2). P. 61: Rüdiger Schöttle. P. 62: Bibliothèque Nationale, Paris (background). P. 63: MOMA/Film Stills Archive; *3e Schrift.* P. 64: Bettmann (background); Stuart Collection, La Jolla. P. 65: NASA; Irene Fortuyn. P. 66: The Institute for Contemporary Art, P.S. 1 Museum, New York. Pps. 66–67: Musée du Louvre, Paris (background). P. 67: Photograph © R.M.N. Musée du Louvre. P. 68: *Veja,* Saõ Paolo (background). P. 69: *Hubert Robert, und*

*Das Bild im Garten,* Gunter Herzog, Wernersche Verlagsgesellschaft, Worms am Rhein; *Veja.* Pps. 70–71: Bernard Bazile, Paris. Pps. 72–73: Harry Walen, M.D., Baltimore (background). P. 75: Harry Walen, M.D.
THE THEATER IN THE GARDEN: FROM ARTIFICE TO ARTIFACT. P. 76: G.P. Putnam and Co., New York. P. 77: Naomi Miller, Boston (2). P. 78: Collection Centre Canadien d'Architecture/Canadian Center for Architecture, Montreal (3). P. 79: La Réunion des Musées Nationaux, Paris; The Library of Congress, Lessing J. Rosenwald Collection, Washington D.C.; Musée Carnavalet, Paris. P. 80: *The Open Air Theater,* Sheldon Cheney, New York, 1918; *Herrenhausen,* Hans Bon Gösseln, Heinr. Feesche Verlag, Hannover, 1971. P. 81: *Herrenhausen, Die Sommerresidenz der Welfen,* Udo von Alvensleben and Hans Reuther, Heinr. Feesche Verlag, Hannover, 1966. P. 82: *Herrenhausen.* P. 83: Dumbarton Oaks, Trustees for Harvard University, Washington D.C.; Naomi Miller. P. 84: Warburg Institute, London. P. 85: Schloss Nymphenburg, Munich (2); Naomi Miller.
GARDEN AS THEATER AS MUSEUM. P. 86: Office for Metropolitan Architecture, Rotterdam; The Print Collection, The Lewis Walpole Library, Yale University (background). P. 87: Kunsthistorisches Institut, Florence. P. 88: Dumbarton Daks. Pps. 88–89: *The Art of Memory,* Frances A. Yates, Ark Paperbacks, London, Melbourne, and Henley, 1984. P. 89: Dumbarton Oaks. P. 90: Yale Center for British Art, Paul Mellon Collection (2). P. 91: Yale Center for British Art; The Metropolitan Museum of Art, Harris Brisban Dick Fund. P. 92: Dan Graham, New York; Bibliothèque Nationale; *The History of Gardens,* Christopher Thacker, Croom Helm, London, 1979; *Jardins en France, 1760–1820,* Caisse Nationale des Monuments Historiques et des Sites, Paris, 1978. P. 93: *The Writing of the Walls,* Anthony Vidler, Princeton Architectural Press, Princeton, 1987; Bettmann (2). P. 94: *The Story of Exhibitions,* Kenneth W. Luckhurst, The Studio Publications, London, 1951 (2). P. 95: Dan Graham; *The Glasshouse,* John Hix, The MIT Press, Cambridge, Massachusetts, 1974; The Mansell Collection, London. P. 96: Carole Kismaric, New York; Jackson, N.J.—Log Flume at Six Flags Great Adventure; Bettmann. P. 97: Dan Graham; *Disneyland: A Degenerate Utopia,* Louis Marin, Johns Hopkins University Press, Baltimore, 1977. P. 98: The Museum of Modern Art, New York; The Equitable Center, New York; Dan Graham. P. 99: Dan Graham. Pps. 100–101: Venturi, Rauch and Scott Brown, Philadelphia (3). P. 102: *Parc-Ville Villette,* Isabelle Auricoste and Hubert Tonka, Edition Champ Vallon, Paris, 1987; Cedric Price, London. P. 103: *Parc-Ville Villette* (background). P. 104: Max Protetch Gallery, New York (2).
ARCHITECTURE THAT SPEAKS: BUILDINGS FOR RITUAL AND DISPLAY. P. 106: The Queens Museum, New York, photograph courtesy General Motors; The Institute of Art History, University of Amsterdam (2). P. 107: Wide World, New York; Culver Pictures Inc., New York (background). P. 108: Bettmann; The Institute of Art History; The United Nations, New York (background). P. 109: The Institute of Art History (3). P. 110: *The Poetics of Gardens,* Charles W. Moore, William J. Mitchell, William Turnbull, Jr., The MIT Press, Cambridge, Massachusetts, 1988 (2); The National Trust. P. 111: *The English Garden,* Edward Hyams, Thames and Hudson, London, 1964; Photographer/The National Trust Photographic Library, England; Photograph Edwin Smith, Gordon Fraser Gallery, Ltd., Wiltshire, England. P. 112: *The Story of Exhibitions*; The John Allwood International Exhibition Collection, Kent; The Library of Congress, courtesy The Queens Museum, New York. P. 113: New York Post, courtesy The Queens Museum; Norman Bel Geddes Collection, Harry Ransom HRC, The

University of Texas at Austin; Photograph Phyllis Bilick, The Queens Museum, New York.
EXHIBITIONITIS: A CONTEMPORARY MUSEUM AILMENT. P. 114: John Weber Gallery, New York. P. 115: The Metropolitan Museum of Art, New York; Marian Goodman Gallery, New York. P. 116: Photograph Fiona Spalding-Smith, National Gallery of Canada/Musée des Beaux-Arts du Canada, Toronto. P. 117: *Princely Gardens,* Kenneth Woodbridge, Rizzoli, New York, 1986; *Hubert Robert et Les Jardins,* Jean de Cayeux, Herscher, Paris, 1987. P. 118: Metro Pictures, New York; Kunsthalle Bern. P. 119: Photograph Neil Frankel, The Metropolitan Museum of Art Shop, New York; *Sesame Street,* The Children's Television Workshop, New York. Pps. 120–121: Musée National d'Art Moderne, Centre Georges Pompidou, Paris (5). P. 122: Johanne Lamoureux. P. 123: Dennis Oppenheim, New York. P. 124: Le Consortium, Dijon. P. 125: Photograph Philippe Degobert, Brussels, Museum van Hedendaagse Kunst, Gent (2). P. 126: Belgian Radio and Television, Brussels.
THE MUSEUM AS AN ANARCHIC EXPERIENCE: A CONVERSATION BETWEEN RICHARD SENNETT AND CHRIS DERCON. P. 128: Kunsthistorisches Institut der Universitat Wien, Vienna. P. 129: *The Ambiguous Image,* Roy Armes, Secker and Warburg, London, 1976; Stadtmuseum, Munich. P. 130: "The Builder 32," 1874; Historisches Museum der Stadt Wien, Vienna (2). P. 131: Bettmann; Bibliothèque Nationale; *Paris 1890's,* Jean Roman, Prentice Hall International, London, 1963. P. 132: *Encyclopedismo in Roma Barocco, Athanasius Kirchner e il Museo del Collegio Romano, tra Wunderkammer e Museo Scientifico*; Bettmann. P. 133: *The Origins of Museums: The Cabinet of Curiosities in Sixteenth- and Seventeenth-Century Europe,* Oliver Impey and Arthur MacGregor, Clarendon Press, Oxford, 1985; *Jardins en France, 1760–1820,* Caisse Nationale des Monuments Historiques et des Sites, Paris, 1978. P. 134: MOMA/Film Stills Archive; Bettmann. P. 135: *London, 2,000 Years of a City and Its People,* (Peter Jackson Collection); John Soane Museum, London. P. 136: Bettmann; The Cone Archives, The Baltimore Museum of Art, Baltimore. P. 137: Kunsthalle Bern; *The Drama Review,* Tisch School of the Arts, New York (2). P. 138: Jannes Linders, Rotterdam; The New Museum of Contemporary Art, New York; Photograph Geoffrey Clements, The Whitney Museum of American Art, New York. P. 139: The Metropolitan Museum of Art; The National Gallery, London; Photograph Tohru Kogure, General Idea, New York
"THEATERGARDEN BESTIARIUM": A BRIEF GUIDE TO THE WORKS IN THE EXHIBITION. Pps. 140–145: Ari Marcopoulos, New York except p. 140, Hans Sonneveld, Brussels (bottom); Pps. 141, (top), 143 (bottom right), 144 (bottom left), and P. 145, Robin Resch, New York; P. 144: David Levinthal, New York (center left); P. 144 Hank Stahler, New York (bottom right).
Pps. 146–159: David Levinthal, New York.
TEXTS WITHOUT A GRAVE. P. 160: Dr. Yuichiro Kojiro, Tokyo (background); *The Art of Memory.* P. 161: The New York Public Library, New York. P. 162: *Staedte, 25 Bildplane von Hermann Bollmann, I,* Bollmann-Bildkarten-Verlag KG, Braunschweig; *The Art of Memory.* P. 163: *The Art of Memory* (2); *Staedte, 25 Bildplane von Hermann Bollmann.* Pps. 164–165: The New York Public Library. Pps. 166–167: The New York Public Library. P. 168: *The Art of Memory* (2). P. 169: The New York Public Library, New York.